SAINT JOSEPH'S HELP

OR

*STORIES OF THE POWER AND EFFICACY
OF SAINT JOSEPH'S INTERCESSION*

From the German of
THE VERY REV. J. A. KELLER, D. D.

Priest of the Diocese of Freibourg,
AUTHOR OF 'SACRED HEART' AND 'MARIA SANCTISSIMA'

THIRD EDITION

Nihil Obstat
RICARDUS A. O'GORMAN, O.S.A.,
CENSOR DEPUTATUS

Imprimatur,
GULIELMUS PRAEPOSITUS JOHNSON,
VICARUS GENERALIS

WESTMONASTERII,
Die 29, Septembris, 1905.

Originally printed by R. & T. Washbourne, LTD.
Republished March 2015 © AMDG
ISBN 978-1508603368

Interior images:
http://medioswww.marysrosaries.com/collaboration/index.php?title=File:Joseph_and_Jesus_001.jpg (Joseph and Jesus 001) Public Domain image.
http://holycardheaven.blogspot.com/2014_02_01_archive.html (The three Hearts of Jesus, Mary & Joseph) Free for use.
http://papastronsaypictures.blogspot.com/ Guardian of Angels and Father St. Joseph image. Free to use for any pious purpose.

Printed in the United States of America

PREFACE.

It is scarcely necessary to recommend a work, whose only object is to make known the power of St. Joseph's intercession with God, and the wonderful favours obtained through his assistance.

The glorious Spouse of the Immaculate Mother, and nursing Father of our Lord Jesus Christ, exercises, after the most holy Virgin Mary, most efficaciously the office of mediator and intercessor before the throne of God.

This is clearly shown in the following relation of wonderful answers to prayers, and graces obtained through his intercession.

This great Saint, so powerful in Heaven, and so full of charity for us, sees daily the number of his devout clients increase, therefore we do not doubt but that this little book will find favour and acceptance, among the many who love to look up to the great Patriarch as their Father and Protector.

We will only add that the following pages are a selection and translation from a larger and most popular German work, compiled by the Very Reverend J. A. Keller, D.D., of the diocese of Freibourg; and that the sources and authorities for every example are given fully in his work.

We have undertaken this translation in the hope that it may be a means of increasing love and devotion to St. Joseph in all who read it, and most especially we trust that it will enkindle in the hearts of children a loving and confiding friendship for this great Patriarch, who was so good a nursing Father to the Divine Child Jesus, and the protector of His childhood and youth.

He will not fail to succour and support those who turn to

him for protection and help, during their sojourn in the Egypt of this world, and when the time of their exile is over he will guide them safely home to the Promised Land of everlasting joy and peace.

O. S. B.

BERGHOLT, *March*, 1888.

CONTENTS.

	PAGE
PREFACE	i

I.
LEGENDS.

1. The Three Lilies of St. Joseph 1
2. The Will and its Executor 8

II.
ST. JOSEPH OUR HELPER IN CORPORAL NECESSITIES.

1. St. Joseph a good Procurator 16
2. St. Joseph helps a Missionary 18
3. St. Joseph in America 19
4. Protection of St. Joseph in Time of War 20
5. St. Joseph Protects a Religious Community 22
6. An Orphanage 25
7. St. Joseph, Protector of School-Children 26
8. St. Joseph's Paschal Candle 27
9. St. Joseph lodges two Missioners 32
10. Origin of the Devotion of the Seven Joys
    and Seven Dolours of St. Joseph 33
11. Safety in Time of Danger 35
12. Under the Protection of St. Joseph 36
13. Protection of St. Joseph during a Pestilence 38
14. Protection of St. Joseph during a Contagious Disease 39
15. St. Joseph all-powerful with God 40
16. 'Speedy Help' 43
17. A Wonderful Cure 43

18. Shelter at Midnight 45
19. Protection in Danger from Fire 46
20. St. Joseph saves a Child from Death by Fire 47
21. Deliverance from Robbers 48
22. An Engineer 50
23. A small Gift towards building a Church in honour of St. Joseph recompensed a hundredfold 51
24. Little Joseph de Malinckroot 52
25. A True Story of the Franco-Prussian War 53
26. St. Joseph answers the Prayer of a Child 56
27. Two True Stories from Westphalia 57
28. A Letter to St. Joseph 59
29. A Good Situation obtained 64
30. The Roll of Money 66
31. St. Joseph helps to build Churches and Schools 67
32. St. Joseph in the Oak 67
33. Cures in Böhle 71
34. Miracles through St. Joseph's Cord 72
35. Confidence in St. Joseph's Intercession rewarded 73
36. 'Arise! You have suffered enough!' 74
37. St. Joseph saves a Child 76
38. Relief from a Pecuniary Embarrassment 78
39. A Lost Paper Found 78
40. The Cord of St. Joseph 79
41. St. Joseph rewards Persevering Confidence 80
42. From Olden Times 82
43. One of St. Joseph's latest Favours 83

III.

ST. JOSEPH OUR HELPER IN SPIRITUAL NECESSITIES.

iv

1. St. Joseph a Good Missioner 88
2. 'Strange' 91
3. A Touching Conversion 92
4. A lost Son found again 94
5. St. Joseph helps in every Distress 95
6. A Good Inspiration 97
7. The little 'First Communicant' 98
8. The Story of a Conversion 102
9. The Successful Examination 104
10. St. Joseph saves two Clerics from the Conscription 105
11. A High Number 106
12. The Last Days of One condemned to Death 107
13. A Miraculous Oil Lamp of St. Joseph 114
14. The Feast of St. Joseph—19th of March 116

IV.
ST. JOSEPH OUR HELPER IN THE HOUR OF DEATH.

1. St. Joseph the Patron of a Happy Death 121
2. The Last Moments of a Papal Zouave 122
3. 'I shall die in the Octave of St. Joseph's Feast' 124
4. 'Behold! St. Joseph is coming to fetch me!' 126
5. An Edifying Death 128
6. St. Joseph does not forget his Clients
   at the Hour of Death 131
7. St. Joseph obtains for the Sick Person the Grace
   of dying in the Arms of Jesus and Mary 135
8. A Favour obtained by the Devout Use of
   St. Joseph's Cord 139
9. A Mysterious Expedition 140
10. A Happy Death 143

11. St. Joseph and a Freemason 145
12. The Apostolate of Prayer 150
13. Protection in the Hour of Death 152
14. How sweet it is to Die with St. Joseph as our Guardian . 154
15. Conversion of a great Sinner through the
    Intercession of St. Joseph 157
16. St. Joseph softens a Hard Heart 161
17. 'Out of my Diary' 166
18. The Picture of St. Joseph's Death 167

V.
ST. JOSEPH OUR HELPER IN EVERY VARIETY OF NECESSITY.

1. Venerate St. Joseph if you wish to Die happily 171
2. Mary and Joseph 171
3. St. Joseph the Teacher of Prayer 172
4. Father Picot de Clorivière 173
5. St. Joseph a Guide on the Road 174
6. Beautiful Death of a faithful client of St. Joseph 175
7. St. Joseph a Master of the Interior Life 175
8. How St. Joseph rewards those who Promote his
    Honour 176

VERSES ON ST. JOSEPH 178

APPENDIX 183

THE CORD OF ST. JOSEPH 183

ST. JOSEPH'S HELP.

I.
Legends.

THE THREE LILIES OF ST. JOSEPH.

NIGHT was slowly giving place to day; that night in which the holy Foster-Father of Our Lord had received the order to fly into Egypt, and the morning sun had already begun to tinge with its ruddy glow the mountain-peaks of Idumea.

Hurriedly and silently the Holy Family pursued their way along the western shore of the Dead Sea, directing their steps towards Egypt. The Divine Child slept; Mary and Joseph communed in secret prayer with God.

After a while, the holy Virgin, sweetly turning herself to Joseph, said:

'Dear Spouse, how it grieves me that, on account of the Child and His Mother, thou shouldst have to undertake so wearisome a journey and bear so heavy a burden.'

'Grieve not,' replied Joseph; 'as for me, I think with wonder on the honour God has done me in choosing me as His instrument in this great undertaking; truly, I know not what I have done to deserve it.'

At these words the Divine Child awoke, and looked up into Joseph's face with eyes beaming with love and confidence; then, raising Himself up on the lap of His Mother, He bowed downwards as if looking and seeking for something on the earth. On the wayside grew white lilies, yet glistening with the morning dew. The holy Joseph understood the meaning of the Child's movement, and stooping, he plucked one of the lilies and offered it to Him. He stretched out His little hand to receive it, showing His childlike joy, as He held it up first to His holy Mother and then to Joseph. At last He held it out to His Foster-Father, and gave it to him, with a look, as if He would say: 'Dost thou know now why God has chosen thee as His instrument?' This look flooded Joseph's heart with gladness, for it filled his soul with a divine grace, which gave him so intimate an understanding of the beauty and sublimity of the angelical virtue of chastity, and of purity of soul, that his heart beat, and his whole body trembled with joy; he held up the lily against the glimmering rosy light of the morning sun, and exclaimed: 'O beautiful lily! yet how far more beautiful the virtue of which thou art the emblem! O lily of a pure heart! Ten such lilies in Sodom and Gomorrah, and they would yet be standing in the midst of verdant plains! O marvellous justice of God against the abominations of sin! Now, in this hour, I understand His ways and the secrets of His judgments!' Thus spoke the holy Joseph in the fullness of his heart, as he walked onwards, and behind the drear and funereal aspect of the Dead

Sea and its fearful shores.

Just then a figure appeared in the far distance; Joseph's heart trembled as he thought of possible danger for the Mother and Child, but, as it approached nearer, he noticed that the habiliments were those of a woman. 'Unclean! unclean!' cried a shrill and mournful voice; it was that of a poor leper, driven out from the abodes of men. Her face was horribly disfigured, and her body was clad in filthy and ragged garments; standing at a distance on the wayside she begged an alms as they passed. Joseph handed the lily to the Child to hold, whilst he drew out a small coin to give to the poor leper; the holy Virgin loosened a little kerchief which she had wrapped round the Divine Child to protect Him from the cold night wind, and handed it also to the distressed creature. Then Joseph, looking at the Child, said: 'Thou also, little one, wouldst certainly wish to give something to this poor beggar if Thou wert not so poor Thyself.' Thereupon the Divine Child held out the lily to the woman, fixing at the same time upon her an earnest but reproachful look.

'See,' said Joseph, 'what the little one gives thee; come and take it.'

The woman took the lily from the hand of the Child.

Can a leper weep? or has not the frightful disease dried up and destroyed the fount of tears? Be that as it may, as this poor leper took the lily, tears streamed from her eyes, and a convulsive sobbing shook her whole frame; she trembled as she staggered to one side, and stood watching the fugitives as they pursued their way until the distance hid them from her sight.

She had been a great sinner, and the leprosy was the punishment of her evil and dissipated life. The Divine Child had given her more than the lily; with it, He had bestowed upon her the grace to see and acknowledge her hateful guilt, and with repentance came the memory of the long-lost innocence of her childhood. As her eyes lost sight of the retreating figures, she covered her face with the kerchief the most holy Virgin had given her, and throwing herself on the ground, gave way to a flood of tears, weeping as if her heart would break.

The day had begun to decline, the western sky was flooded with a gold and crimson tint; but as the sun sank below the horizon, a cool, fresh wind blew from the west.

The holy Mother pressed her little one closer to her bosom, and drew her blue mantle tighter around Him; she missed now the protecting kerchief which in the morning she had given to the poor leper. Joseph noticed her with pain, and there came a temptation to the poor, tired, houseless, anxious man, and he sighed as he said:

'It will be very hard, O Mary, for poor fugitives and exiles such as we, to have to find food, clothing, and shelter. Soon the little sum of money we brought with us will be expended; perhaps before we reach our destination we shall be penniless; and even when we reach the term of our flight, what means shall we find to provide for the future? Poor Mother—poor Child!'

Anxiously the Mother looked at her Virgin Spouse, but she had to turn quickly to the Child, Who strove to raise Himself in her arms, and was stretching out His little hands towards the ground.

Again were the wayside lilies the object of His desires, and again did the holy Joseph pick one, and, as he handed it to Him, he received one of those wonderful looks from His Divine eyes that penetrated the inmost depths of his soul.

'Pardon, pardon, Mary!' he exclaimed; 'I have indeed spoken foolishly.' And he began at once to sing the 90th Psalm: 'He that dwelleth in the help of the Most High, shall abide under the protection of the God of Heaven.'

As he continued it, the Child fell asleep again in His Mother's arms; and before Joseph had concluded the Psalm, he espied in the distance a little lowly hut, or cottage, towards which he at once directed his steps, resolving to seek there a shelter during the night for the Mother and Child.

The inmates of the cottage, though they accorded the usual Eastern hospitality, looked gloomily at them as they entered; and the master of the house, approaching Joseph, said with a surly voice:

'Here you may indeed enter; but poverty and misery are the only dwellers in this abode, and despair is already on the threshold!'

'My friend,' answered the holy Joseph, as he showed him the lily which he held with the pilgrim's staff in his hand, 'behold this flower of the field: it soweth not, neither does it reap; it builds itself no shelter, and yet it always holds its beautiful head erect to the sun; care never bows it to the earth. Raise up also your head, for the same God Who cares for this lily, cares also for you.'

The impression these words produced was most wonderful, for the grace of the little Christ-Child was with them and with the second lily of St. Joseph.

The Holy Family rested for the night under this sheltering roof, and spent the evening in conversation full of comfort and consolation for those who had received them. In the morning they rose early to continue their flight, but before leaving, their host begged of St. Joseph the lily that he held in his hand, and refused all other payment or gifts. He placed the lily in a vase of water, and as long as he lived it never faded or withered.

Has it ever chanced to you, dear reader, at any time to stand in a garden, as the evening shadows fell and the sombre veil of twilight began to envelop the earth as with a pall? At such a moment the lily flower appears to stand out like a corona of light, its glistening white petals breaking through the darkness.

Well, then, listen now to the story of Joseph's third lily.

Many days had passed since St. Joseph had left the lily in the hands of the owner of the desert dwelling, yet still the fugitives were hastening on their weary way. They were now nearing the frontiers of Egypt; already from a curve in the road they had seen in the distance the dome of an idolatrous temple, rising from the midst of dwelling-houses, and shining as it caught the rays of the setting sun. But the holy Joseph had a very sad heart, all the more because, as the sun set, a thick darkness began to spread itself over the earth, and it became almost impossible to distinguish the path they had to take. Laying his hand on the bridle of the ass which carried their little burdens, he sighed and said:

'If only we had a torch!'

Just then the Divine Child, Who was sleeping in His Mother's arms, awoke, and stretching out His little hands, seemed to seek something from the ground. At once the holy Joseph looked and saw an object white and shining, gleaming amid the dark green on the wayside. Again it was a lily. He plucked it, and handed it to the Child, but as he gave it into His hands, behold! from the corolla of the flower a dazzling white light streamed forth, which spread itself all around, whilst a small white Host, with a tiny shining red cross in its centre, floated just above the flower petals.

The clear, bright light fell upon the pathway, and made the journey now quite easy. The Divine Child held out the wonderful lily-torch to St. Joseph, who, with renewed courage, and joy, pursued his way, but silently, for a holy fear and astonishment possessed his whole soul.

This light, which was a mysterious revelation of that Food of Angels wherewith the Lord feeds the souls of men, served as a guide for the Divine Child, on His entrance into that land, where of old the people of God had been fed with heavenly manna; and this image of the most adorable Sacrifice, through which the Name of God, as the Prophet had foretold, 'should be great among the nations,' entered, shining brightly, into the idolatrous city, to oppose its light to the darkness of the idolatrous worship of an unbelieving people.

Soon the Holy Family found themselves in the midst of an Egyptian city, and were passing before the great Temple whose shining dome they had beheld from the distance. The light from the radiant lily fell on the huge misshapen and grotesque idol, carved in white marble, that was in front of the temple gates, and in this pure light it was changed into an object black and murky as the dark night. A priest of the idol stood beside it, and a ray of the Divine light of grace fell also upon his heart; raising his voice he exclaimed prophetically:

'Oh Lily, thou hast come to conquer the Lotus!'*

Then turning to the Holy Family, he said:

'Strangers, whomsoever you may be, a God is with you, and His light enlightens you,' and immediately closing the gates of the temple, he disappeared into its dark recesses.

---

* The lotus flower was the symbol of Egyptian idolatry.

The Holy Family had in the meantime moved onwards, and reached a house before whose entrance a lamp was burning. Here the lily suddenly emitted a flame of marvelous brilliancy, illuminating the whole house as it stood before them. The holy Joseph took this for a sign that he should here seek and find shelter. He accordingly approached the door, and in this domicile the Holy Family found a home at the commencement of their sojourn in the idolatrous land of Egypt. But the lily became invisible; it had been taken by an Angel's hand and laid on the Mount of Calvary.

This, dear reader, is the parable of the three lilies of St. Joseph, but you must note well its signification, and remember the following lesson that it teaches.

A pure heart is the greatest of treasures, and a pledge of predestination; its loss the most deplorable misery and unhappiness.

A pure heart is a source of consolation and confidence in God.

A pure heart is victorious over the devil, idolatry, and superstition, and is the special and intimate friend of Jesus in the holy Sacrament of the Altar.

St. Joseph beseeches you never to forget these lessons.

THE WILL AND ITS EXECUTOR.

A Legend from the Spanish of Fernan Caballero.

PAY attention, dear children, and I will tell you a story; a story which, perhaps, may never have really happened, but which is well known and often related, and which, even if it never occurred, will do both your heart and your soul good to hear.

Once upon a time there lived a pious honest man, who

worked as a carpenter; he was with his whole heart devoted to St. Joseph, the patron of his trade. St. Joseph was, as you know, a carpenter, and therefore, from the earliest times, all mechanics, and especially carpenters, have honoured him and considered him as their model and patron.

The Capuchin Fathers once gave an order to our carpenter to make an altar for the chapel of St. Joseph in their convent, and he succeeded so well that the whole town came to see it, and admired the skilfull manner in which he had handled his tools, especially in the delicate carvings, in which he had represented in a most lively and touching manner the humility and love of the Man-God, Who had not disdained, during His mortal life, the humble dwelling of a poor but industrious carpenter.

It is one of those peculiarities of men that things which they can see with their eyes make more impression on them than those things which they hear, and this is one of the reasons why our holy Mother the Church gives, and has given from the earliest times, so much encouragement to all visible representations in her Temples of the mysteries of our holy Faith.

But to return to our carpenter: As years rolled on, trouble in many shapes visited his little home; first his wife died, then he lost all his children except one daughter, he himself fell sick, and as he had grown old and weak, he could do very little work. At last he became completely blind, and consequently incapable of earning anything for his subsistence.

He bore all these trials and contradictions with the greatest patience and resignation to the Divine Will, never losing his confidence in God, or his trust in his holy patron, Saint Joseph.

His good daughter nursed and tended him as well as she

could, but this left her very little time to spare in which to earn anything for their support; consequently she was obliged to part, one by one, with all the little furniture and necessaries in the house, in order to provide food and fuel; so that in a short time they were reduced to the extremity of poverty and distress.

In this sorrowful condition the old carpenter felt his end approaching, and desiring to die as a good Christian, he received all the last Sacraments, and prepared his soul for its passage into eternity.

Then, calling his daughter, he desired her to go and fetch a notary, in order that he might make his last will and testament.

'*You* want to make a will, father!' exclaimed the astonished girl. 'Why! what have you that you can leave? Are we not already reduced to the direst poverty and want?'

'Never mind, my daughter, but go quickly and do as I bid thee.'

'The fever is making him delirious,' said the poor girl, wringing her hands in her distress; but still she dared not disobey, so she went out to fulfill his wishes.

The notary, on hearing her request, raised his eyes with surprise, and smiling said to himself:

'Ah! this old carpenter, who appeared so poor, has, after all, money to leave; he must have become a miser in his old age, and his poverty has only been a cloak to hide his treasures. Well, a death-bed brings many secrets to light. We shall see now to whom he will leave all that he has saved!'

Saying this, he put on his hat, and taking up a roll of parchment, ink, and a pen, he prepared to follow the girl to the old man's house.

After a few minutes' walk he arrived at the poor cottage,

and entered the room where the old carpenter lay sick; a wretched bed and one chair constituted the whole of the furniture of the apartment.

The notary seated himself, and having unrolled and spread out his parchment on the bed, as there was no table, he took out his pen, dipped it in the ink, and wrote the usual form at the head of the will:

'In the Name of the Most Holy Trinity.'

Then he looked up to the old man for his instructions how to proceed. The carpenter with an effort raised himself a little, and in a weak and trembling voice began to dictate:

'I bequeath my soul to God, my body to the earth, and I name my holy Patron, St. Joseph, as the guardian of my daughter, and executor of this my last will and testament.'

Having finished these words, he sank back on his pillow, and with one deep sigh his soul passed peacefully into eternity. The notary, who had expected something very different from this, rose in consternation and affright. Without noticing the poor weeping girl, who knelt beside the bed, he rapidly collected together his parchment, ink, and pen, and left the house more speedily than he had entered.

The poor daughter now felt all the bitterness of her loss. She was alone in the world, and so poor that she knew not how she should be able to provide a shroud and coffin, and all that was requisite for the Christian burial of her poor father. Clasping her hands together, she bowed her head on the bed and wept unrestrainedly.

So she remained until she was aroused by a knock at the door. She rose to open it, and a noble but aged man with a most kind and friendly countenance entered the little room. He wore a plain coat, was wrapped in a dark mantle, and carried a staff in his hand.

'Comfort thyself, my child,' he said to the desolate girl; 'be not troubled; I will take care of everything; leave all to me, and I will see all prepared for your father's burial.'

Then, after a few more words of encouragement and comfort, he went out, and soon again returned with men bearing a coffin and all that was needful. The priests also came, and on the next day the poor carpenter had an honourable and Christian funeral. The noble stranger himself followed the coffin to the grave as chief mourner, and remained to see the body consigned to the earth.

After having performed this last service for the deceased, the stranger turned his steps to one of the principal streets of the town and knocked for admission at the house of a rich and well-known merchant. He announced himself as one who had important business to transact, and when the merchant came to him he at once said:

'Do you remember a severe storm at sea which you encountered a few years ago, off the coast of Spain, in which you were in great danger of losing not only your vessel and merchandise, but also your life, and the lives of all the crew?'

'Yes, I remember it well,' answered the astonished merchant, 'but how could you know of it?'

'Do you remember,' continued the stranger, 'a vow which you then made, that if God would save you from that peril, you would seek out the poorest and most virtuous maiden, and espouse her as your wife?'

'How!' exclaimed the still more surprised merchant, 'how is it possible that you should know this? Never in my life have I mentioned to any person this secret promise I made to God!'

'Have you still the intention to fulfil your vow?' continued the venerable stranger, without noticing the question of the other.

'Yes,' he replied, 'yes; and I am grieved that I have so long delayed to perform what I promised to God.'

'Will you then allow me to introduce you to the poorest, but also the most virtuous maiden in this town?'

'By all means; my heart feels so strange and yet so strong a feeling of confidence in you, that I am resolved to be guided in this matter entirely by your counsel and advice.'

The next morning the merchant, accompanied by the noble stranger, went to the dwelling of the desolate and bereaved daughter. The poor girl was in the greatest distress, for already the landlord had given her notice to leave, as he feared she would be unable to pay the rent for the house.

'Weep not, my child,' said her unknown benefactor, 'you need have no anxiety for the future; see, this gentleman who has come with me, he will take care of you. He is good and pious, and blessed with worldly means; he is willing to marry you, and as his wife he will protect and support you.'

The maiden willingly agreed to this proposal, and all the necessary arrangements for the betrothal were made.

When the time of mourning had elapsed the marriage took place with much rejoicing and solemnity, and as all were assembled at the wedding-feast, the newly-married pair begged of their benefactor, who was sitting in a friendly manner in their midst, that would be pleased to tell them who he was, in order that they might know to whom they owed so much happiness, and so many benefits.

The venerable stranger rose, and with a sweet and pleasant smile thus addressed all who were present:

'I am Joseph, who received from God the grace and dignity

of being the husband and guardian of Mary, and the nursing Father and protector of the Divine Child. Thy pious father, my daughter, consecrated himself and his whole life to my honour, service and devotion, and on his death-bed he appointed me the executor of his last will and testament. I have now punctually fulfilled all. His good soul I presented to God, his body I committed to the earth, and as thy guardian I have also faithfully provided for thy happiness and well-being.'

Whilst he spoke these words the roof of the room seemed to open, and a light, brilliant and rosy as the early morning sunrise, and clear as the day, streamed all around. In the midst of this heavenly light appeared a glorious Child who called, saying:

'Come, Father, come, Mother wants you.'

At this vision the pious couple and all the wedding guests sank on their knees and received with folded hands, and eyes flowing with tears, the blessing of the Saint, who, with his eyes fixed on the bride and bridegroom, took the hand of the Divine Child and held it raised in blessing above them, until his figure disappeared, and was lost in the blue sky of the heavens.

Now, dear children, what do you think of this story?

I will tell you one thing, which it ought to impress on your minds, and that is the great benefits which God bestows on those who have confidence in the intercession of St. Joseph.

For even if it never really occurred exactly as the legend has come down to us, yet, certainly, it could have happened, for there is nothing derogatory in it to the honour of the Saint, and it brings before us the consoling thought that in the midst of the grievous and multiplied trials of life, God sends us help through the means and intercession of His Saints, only we must remember this help may not always be granted to us in such a visible and miraculous manner.

II.
St. Joseph our helper in Corporal Necessities.

1. St. Joseph is a Good Procurator.

A MORE holy or venerable cloister has never existed in this world, than that in the little town of Nazareth, eighteen hundred years ago. It has become the ideal and perfect model of all religious communities, and its three holy inhabitants, Jesus, Mary and Joseph, are the mirror of all souls consecrated to God, which they ought daily to contemplate, in order to mould according to these Divine hearts, their own life, their souls, their whole hearts.

Yes, truly, this poor little hut of Nazareth has witnessed in their highest perfection all those virtues which form the real foundation of a life consecrated to God. Poverty, chastity, obedience, mortification, manual labour, humility and self-denial, charity and sacrifice, prayer and contemplation; all these sweet and heavenly flowers have never flourished more luxuriantly or beautifully than in the house of Nazareth, the first Christian cloister upon earth.

The head of this little community, the glorious St. Joseph, has been at all times an especial friend, patron and protector of all houses and souls consecrated to God, and still to this day often manifests this fatherly predilection in a remarkable manner, even sometimes condescending to work miracles to prove his paternal care and compassion for Religious, when suffering distress of any kind.

The following simple but touching anecdote of the Franco-German war, in 1870, is an example of his kind and powerful protection. I know not how it is that amongst all the instances of blessing conferred by St. Joseph in these our times, none has impressed me more than the occurrence I am about to relate.

When the terrible siege of Metz began, there was a large and flourishing convent belonging to the Dames du Sacré-Cœur, situated in the suburbs of the town. They were of course obliged to dismiss all their pupils, and instead of these innocent children, whom they had been teaching to lead good and happy lives in piety, diligence and peace, they were forced to harbour and feed more than one hundred soldiers.

When, at last, the siege was over, misery and distress, instead of being also at an end, seemed then only to begin in sad earnest. In the convent, as elsewhere, even the necessaries of life were wanting, and the inmates knew not how to obtain them. But instead of being discouraged, the good Religious placed their confidence all the more firmly in God, and unanimously resolving to give themselves unreservedly into the hands of St. Joseph, they with child-like simplicity devised the following plan.

During recreation hour, one of the nuns made a little sack, into which was put a morsel of everything they most needed — a potato, a bit of wood, a scrap of bread, a tiny bottle of oil, etc.

This sack was then laid at the feet of St. Joseph's statue, as it were to make the Saint fully and clearly aware of their wants.

And it did indeed seem as if his tender heart could not resist this appeal, for the very next morning arrived at the door of the convent a man with two heavily-laden wagons of wood.

The Superioress, who naturally knew nothing about it,

explained to the good man that she had neither ordered wood, nor had she any money to pay for it. But he would not allow himself to be sent away, and began to unload his wagons, answering that he had been desired to say: 'This is the wood of St. Joseph, destined for the convent of the Sacré-Cœur.'

Who cannot imagine the joyous astonishment of the nuns at so quick and generous an answer to their prayers?

But their confidence was to be still more rewarded, as oil was much wanting. The Sister whose duty it was each evening to walk all through the passages and rooms of the large house, besought St. Joseph to supply her with the necessary oil for the lamp which she was obliged to carry with her, as her duty occupied more than half an hour, promising, in return, that if he would grant her request she would burn a light in his honour. And now behold what happened: the little lamp, which ordinarily needed refilling three times in the week, suddenly appeared to become inexhaustible.

Night after night did this good Sister make her rounds, carrying the wonderful lamp, which always remained so full that not a drop more oil could be poured into it.

When this miracle first became known, it had already continued for thirteen months; whether it still goes on I cannot say, but I do know that these are only two out of the many other signal favours accorded by St. Joseph to this religious house.

2. St. Joseph helps a Missionary.

During the time that I was building my church in 1879, being in the utmost trouble and distress about my debts, I began a Novena to St. Joseph nine days before his feast, hoping that he would help me. On the first day of this Novena, I happened to visit a neighbouring brother priest, and told him that I was now sure of the money I needed, as I had placed the affair in the hands of St. Joseph. This otherwise good and pious priest answered in a somewhat satirical tone: 'Oh! then you will certainly receive something handsome—how much do you want?' I replied that I must get at least £75: and then the conversation changed.

I continued the Novena, but obtained nothing. At last, on the eighth day, arrived a donation of £7 10s. The next day, the 19th of March was a Sunday. After the early Mass, I sent as usual to the post-office, and judge of my joy and gratitude to find there awaiting me a money order for £67 10s., just the sum I required to complete the £75. Who could have felt greater happiness than I did, as I laid the money on the altar before the statue of St. Joseph, and thanked our Divine Lord and His Foster-Father for their wonderful help.

3. St. Joseph in America.

A filiation of Dominican Nuns from the convent of Holy Cross at Ratisbon, in Bavaria, went to America, and settled in Green Bay, in the north of Wisconsin. Their little house in the commencement was very poor. One of the nuns relates:

We were at that time so poor that often we had neither money, nor firing, nor even food. Once, on a very cold evening, there was not a single piece of wood in the house to light the fire for the next morning. We did again that night what we had often successfully tried in like emergencies; before we went to bed, we fervently invoked St. Joseph's assistance in our distress.

Suddenly, at midnight, we were all awaked by a heavy rumbling noise, and then we heard sounds as if a wagon of wood was being unloaded.

Hastily arising, we went downstairs and found this indeed to be the case. A Dutch farmer whom we knew, and who resided about four miles from our house, was standing there, and in reply to our question, how he happened to think of bringing us wood at such an unusual time, especially as we had not ordered it, only replied, that he could not tell—an interior voice had urged him to set off at once, as the nuns were in great want of it.

Whose voice could this have been, save that of our powerful protector?

4. Protection of St. Joseph in Time of War.

The following passage we have extracted from the 'Propagateur de la dévotion à St. Joseph et à la Sainte Famille,' and it may tend to increase more and more the devotion to the glorious Foster-Father of our Lord:

We have all heard of the devastations, the horrible sacrileges and the murders committed in those unfortunate provinces which were ravaged by the Garibaldians. Their rapacity and cruelty were especially excited against religious houses, so that we do not hesitate to consider the following fact as a miracle worked by St. Joseph.

A Jesuit Father at Rome writes on the 28th of October, 1867, as follows:

'Reverend Father,

'An invasion of the Garibaldians was hourly expected. Six of our Fathers returned from Tivoli to Rome, eleven others remained in Tivoli, where for eight days they were surrounded by brigands.

'In their distress, the Fathers made a vow to perform a solemn Triduo in honour of St. Joseph, if he would vouchsafe to protect them.

'The vile Garibaldians had occupied all the religious houses except one; and while our schoolrooms were unoccupied, except by the comfortable beds provided for the Zouaves, who shortly before had been quartered there, the Garibaldians were content to remain in the neighbourhood with no better accommodation than straw for their night's lodgings.

'No kind of contribution was demanded from us, indeed, the only visit they made us was in order to make an offering to the Father Rector of a book carried off from the library of the seminary, which they had plundered.

'On the last day of their stay, they sent to ask for four barrels of wine, which we gave them; but on the first tidings of the defeat of Mentana, they hastily decamped, leaving our four barrels quite untouched.

'On Sunday Father M—— came with a deputation of three of our pupils to assist at the conclusion of our three days' devotion in honour of St. Joseph.

'The Triduo had also the same happy result as a successful Mission, for on the last day there were at least one thousand communicants.

'The news that we had escaped so fortunately excited the greatest astonishment in Rome, and His Holiness Pope Pius IX. vouchsafed on this occasion to grant us a Plenary Indulgence.'

5. St. Joseph protects a Religious Community.

In the year 1871 the population of Angoulême was in great anxiety, fearing an outbreak of the revolutionary party which had already committed such outrages in Marseilles and Lyons.

The religious communities, terrified at the approach of the storm, which was sure to fall most fiercely on them, implored the succour and protection of Almighty God and His Saints.

Among these communities was one whose Superioress had a great devotion to St. Joseph, and after offering to him many fervent prayers for the safety of her children, she felt inspired to fasten to the outer door of the convent a picture of St. Joseph, with the clearly expressed intention that he should take upon himself the office of guardian of the community.

She did this with such complete confidence that afterwards, in order to encourage the Sisters, she said to them simply:

'Fear nothing, my children; we have St. Joseph as our sentinel at the door; under such protection all is secure.'

By and by evening came on, and the most threatening rumours spread through the town. Suspicious-looking people were seen in the streets, the crowd continued to increase, and finally, about two hours after sunset, a savage mob, shouting, blaspheming, and vociferating dreadful threats against the Religious, set out in the direction of this convent, which it was feared they would at once attack. And these forebodings proved only too true, for the miserable, misguided wretches soon began their malicious work. With heavy stones, clubs, or any other implements they could lay hands upon, they endeavoured to force open the door.

The Sisters had already gone to rest with the exception of the Superioress and her Mother-Assistant, and they kept watch in prayer before an image of St. Joseph. But at the first sound of this terrific uproar, one and all started out of bed, and rushed downstairs. They were met by their Superioress, Mother N——, who calmly desired them to retire to rest again, assuring them that the honour of their heavenly Protector being at stake, he would be sure to save them.

Supernatural obedience prevailed over human fear, and the poor nuns retired again to their cells, although to sleep even 'with one eye' (as they say in Germany), was out of the question, for it seemed as if all the demons of hell were yelling and raging around their convent.

Meanwhile Mother N——went down to the hall or vestibule to ascertain how the work of destruction was going on; and to her alarm she already could see great cracks and fissures in the door. Hastily returning to the Oratory, she and the Mother-Assistant again most fervently commended the Community to the care of their blessed Guardian.

Then once more descending the staircase she found this time that the fastenings of the door were almost destroyed. A few more blows, and their savage enemies would have gained entrance, to wreak their inhuman vengeance on these helpless victims.

With more earnestness than ever, yet with increased confidence and peace of mind, did this heroic Religious again recommend herself to St. Joseph; when suddenly, in a moment, all was silent!

What does it mean? Her heart answers her that her prayers have been heard. She rose from her knees, and for the third time went downstairs, hardly able to believe her own ears, and thinking that she must be labouring under a delusion. But no! nothing was to be heard. She looked at the door, and to her surprise saw that half of it was in ruins, and yet no one had entered! She dared even to go farther, and looked through the large opening into the street; but where lately there had been an immense crowd, now not a single human being was to be seen, only the reflection of the street gas-lamp quietly shining on the opposite wall.

'Well, Deo gratias, it is all right,' she said to herself, 'now we must thank St. Joseph.'

No sooner said than done, and after a most fervent act of gratitude and thanksgiving, both she and the Mother-Assistant went peacefully to bed, and we trust also to sleep.

The next morning dawned clear and bright. Except the ruined door, no sign remained of the last night's alarm, and if it had not been for this silent but eloquent witness, the nuns might almost have persuaded themselves that the events of the previous few hours had been more a dreadful dream than a reality.

During the course of the day Mother N——was called to the guest-room to see a pious lady who had come to express her condolence and sympathy with the Community for the terrors of the past night. Then she asked the Superioress if she knew the person whose appearance had frightened away the impious crew in a moment. Mother N——replied that she only saw that the door was very nearly destroyed, but that she knew nothing of the person whom she mentioned. The lady then related the following account:

'When I heard that awful noise I went to the window in a house opposite to the convent door, to observe the frightful scene from behind a shutter. The thought of the inevitable suffering for these Spouses of our Divine Lord seemed to pierce my heart, and I had hardly the strength or courage to look on at the work of destruction. As I gazed I saw a tall man of very noble deportment and venerable exterior come out of the little street which bounds your house at the side. With slow steps he approached the crowd, apparently as a spectator, neither speaking a word nor making the least sign. But truly he had not come merely to look. Scarcely was his presence perceived than the wretches were struck dumb, and seemed as if they could not hurry away quickly enough. Surely he must have been a man of great importance, whose mere appearance was sufficient to frighten away this band of human devils. Who could he have been?

'Let us thank Divine Providence,' answered the Superioress, 'Whom it has pleased to deliver us by the means of St. Joseph from such an extremity of peril.'

Go to St. Joseph; in his hand is placed the welfare of nations and countries. Entrust therefore all things you can to his protection, then will it be well with you in time and eternity.

6. An Orphanage.

Not long ago, the good Superioress of a Franciscan Convent was in great distress. We do not know her real name, so we will call her Mother F——.

Well, her trouble was this; the nuns had undertaken the care of an Orphanage, and they endeavoured to bring up as many destitute little children as possible, in the love and fear of God. But for some time, from different causes, they had been growing poorer and poorer, and now Mother F——was told that she must send away some of her much loved orphans, as she had not the means of supporting them. Her motherly heart bled at the thought of turning these little ones of Christ adrift again into a world of sin and misery, and she resolved at least to delay the evil hour for some days; meanwhile with the most ardent fervour imploring the assistance of St. Joseph, the powerful protector of youth, to guide and help her in this sad difficulty.

Her request was not made in vain. The very next Wednesday an unknown person sent her a considerable sum of money for the sustenance of her poor children. The Wednesday following arrived another present to rejoice the heart of the good Mother, in the shape of a large parcel of old clothing, sent by a Tertiary of St. Francis, for the use of the orphans. And on the third Wednesday she received again a large sum of money, sent quite unexpectedly by a relation of one of the children. Thanks be to St. Joseph.

7. St. Joseph, Protector of School-Children.

This is another story for the children. It was contributed by the Sisters of St. Joseph, and shows wonderfully the care this loving Foster-Father takes of the little ones entrusted to him.

The children were in school in their various classes, when suddenly, with a frightful crash, down fell from its stand a very large and heavy blackboard, crushing in its fall several of the younger children, who were not more than four or five years of age. It is impossible to describe the terror of the nuns in charge of the classes! Trembling with fear they raised the blackboard, expecting to find the children killed, or at least seriously injured when to their intense joy, instead of the sight they dreaded, they beheld rosy, laughing faces. The little ones were unhurt, and not even frightened under their heavy wooden cover, thanks to Our Lord, Our Lady, and St. Joseph. The children had been each day taught to recommend themselves to their care and protection before two statues placed on pedestals in the schoolroom.

The fact just related was of more consequence in Germany than it would, perhaps, have been in our country; as there, the enemies of the Church are always endeavouring to deprive the Religious of the education of youth, replacing them by seculars; and they would have been sure to avail themselves of such an accidental circumstance to form a pretext for the expulsion of the nuns from this school.

8. St. Joseph's Paschal Candle.

We learned the following from the 'Lilies of Mary,' in Naples:

A good country priest who had a great devotion to St. Joseph found himself one day in trouble.

The feast of the Resurrection of Our Lord was at hand, and he had neither a Paschal candle prepared, nor the money to buy one. His three hundred parishioners were so poor, that all, more or less, had difficulty to support themselves, and took with thanks the small alms their pastor, nearly as poor as themselves, was able to offer them. A collection in church, therefore, would have been useless, for how could these poor people give what they did not possess?

Some time previously, this good priest had formed the grand idea of re-building, without any assistance from his flock, the parish church, which was falling into ruins, and, like Solomon, to erect a temple to the Most High.

His determination being taken, he girded his pilgrim's dress, and knocked first at the door of the Bishop. A lovingly given blessing, and, as a foundation stone, a sum of 1,000 lire (about £40), were the result of this visit. A better beginning could not have been expected. For three years did this zealous priest continue his laborious wanderings: often over muddy roads or slippery ice, through rain and frost, or exposed to the heat of the burning sun, or what comes still harder to human nature, to humiliations and contradictions of all kinds. After enduring all these trials with the greatest patience and cheerfulness, he at length returned to his flock, and one Sunday morning announced to them the joyful news that their church was about to be rebuilt.

Quickly he summoned architects, builders, bricklayers, masons, carpenters, painters—even sculptors—and after unheard-of labours, and numberless sacrifices, the courageous priest at last saw his dream realized. The Bishop came to consecrate the new House of God, and the Holy Sacrifice was offered in it.

But the unwearied zeal of the good pastor created for him new duties and fresh toils. He now longed to gild the altar, to silver the candlesticks, to procure a new pulpit, to erect a confessional, etc. Thus the little money which remained over from the building was soon expended; and so it came to pass that, at the time our story began, Easter was fast approaching, his purse was completely empty, and there was no Paschal candle!

What could be done?

Should he buy one on credit?

No, decidedly not! It was one of his inviolable principles, never to go into debt.

So, instead, he began a Novena to St. Joseph, under whose patronage the church was erected; for ought not that glorious

Patriarch to aid those who, following his example, provide a lodging for that same Lord Jesus Christ, Who could find no shelter in the city of Bethlehem?

This Novena ended on the 25th of March, which this year fell on Maundy Thursday. This true imitator of the poverty of Christ had now nothing more to sell. He had parted with his watch; with his silver teapot, which had been given to him by his mother on the day of his installation as parish priest; with his armchair, the gift of one of his great friends at the seminary; with the cushion, which his sister had so beautifully embroidered for him: all—all was gone with the exception of an ivory crucifix, the legacy of a dearly-beloved friend; all had been turned into money for the completion of his great work.

On the morning of Maundy Thursday, a strange idea presented itself to his mind. There was living in a castle, about fifteen miles distant, a Jew, a retired banker, who was immensely rich. The good priest had never before asked an alms of him, because it was well known that he never gave alms to a Christian, much less to a priest.

One moment the holy man hesitated; it was not at all agreeable to go to the Jew, but he considered this thought as an inspiration of St. Joseph; and, possessing the simplicity of a child, to receive an inspiration from God and to obey it, was like one action for him.

After holy Mass, he set out, saying the Rosary on his way. Now the 'Kleine Pastor,' as his parishioners fondly called him, besides being a very spiritual theologian and a saint, was also a poet.

Like St. Francis of Assisi, he delighted to entertain himself with the beasts and the birds, and as he went along the road, the wonders of creation and the power and wisdom of their

Creator, evinced even in the little wayside flowers, were to his pure mind rich and sublime lessons.

When he entered the castle court he met the carriage of the master, who cast a cold and contemptuous glance on this uninvited guest, who even dared to walk into his private grounds.

The step of the priest became very slow!—

The banker had just sat down to his dinner, when a servant entered asking whether he would receive that poor man whom he had just before met.

'Give him a piece of bread,' replied the master, 'and tell him to leave me in peace.'

'But he insists on seeing you, and speaking with you,' continued the servant.

'Then he may wait.'

The good priest, not daring to sit down on one of the velvet chairs in the saloon, and seeing a little bench in the court, humbly retired to it, fervently beseeching St. Joseph to help him. After dinner the lord of the castle lighted a cigar, and again his servant, who felt pity for the poor little man who looked so tired, and was all covered with dust, ventured to remind his master.

'Will your lordship now receive that poor man?'

'What!—is he still here? then let him come in, but tell him to be short.'

The priest saluted the Jew reverentially and made known his request. The banker broke out into a short laugh, which seemed a bad presage. Was it not indeed strange, almost impertinent, to ask from him, a Jew, the means of celebrating the Resurrection of Him Whom his ancestors had crucified?

But how was it possible to be angry with this beggar, who

was so gentle and humble?

Herr N——, who always liked to find out the motives of people's actions, was surprised that this priest seemed quite unconscious of having come to just the wrong person.

He already began to take the mistake more favourably. On the other hand, he thought it a good opportunity to learn what kind of a man a priest might be.

'We will see,' he said, assuming again his rough and severe deportment; 'sit down, sir, and tell me your story.'

The humble priest, who was not accustomed to speak about himself, felt for a moment very perplexed. Nevertheless he obeyed, and with winning sweetness described his dear home, in which he had been the eldest of ten children. Then he spoke of the seminary, his second home, which was in a manner like the vestibule of the Sanctuary; and he became wonderfully animated at the remembrance of those happy times. Then he described his parish, and the church as it was now (by whose merits it had become so, he did *not* tell),—and spoke about the piety of his parishioners, and of the peace of the solitude of his country life, which he dedicated to God and His creatures.

What touching eloquence did not God and his good Angel place on his lips as he portrayed all these things!

Scarcely had he finished when Herr N——arose, and with reverence and emotion said: 'Sir, allow me to express to you my sympathy and admiration. I do not know which of us two possesses the truth, but I envy you. You are happy in a faith which inspires such great sacrifices. You shall have a Paschal candle, Reverend Father, and from this moment I give you an unlimited credit for your church, for your poor, and for yourself. Consent to make *me* your banker.'

'Kleine Pastor,' who left the castle in a carriage, carried in his pocket a purse well filled with bank notes.

Without doubt St. Joseph had interposed here, and the whole neighbourhood had much to say about the splendid Paschal candle given by Herr N— —.

Every day the priest prays in church for his generous benefactor, and every Sunday he visits him,—and it is fully believed by the parishioners that St. Joseph will not stop half way in the work he has begun, but will certainly lead this man, who so willingly complied with his desires, to the true faith.

9. St. Joseph lodges two Missioners.

The chronicles of the Franciscan Fathers relate the following occurrence:

Father Jerome Vistoya, a Capuchin and Apostolic Missioner, who was especially devoted to St. Joseph, went with another Father of his Order to Venice, whence by order of the Holy See he was to embark for the island of Candia.

It was summer, and to avoid the intolerable heat of the sun they travelled by night, and so it happened once that they lost their way.

After straying about for some time, exhausted and hungry, they knelt down and invoked Jesus, Mary and Joseph for assistance.

When they had finished their prayer they saw in the distance the glimmer of a lamp, and following its light, they soon reached a little house which they found inhabited by an old man, with his wife and child, all of dignified and beautiful in appearance.

They introduced themselves as travellers, who had lost their way, and begging for shelter, were received with the utmost kindness and hospitality.

When they awoke the next morning, after a good night's rest, they found themselves lying in a meadow, and they saw not the slightest trace of the cottage or its inmates.

Then these good Fathers doubted no longer that they had been entertained by the Holy Family itself, and thanked God gratefully for so excellent a protection.

The learned Eckius, in his homilies on St. Joseph, says: 'Let all who have to undertake dangerous journeys, and travel through hostile countries, recommend themselves to St. Joseph for his protection and security.'

10. Origin of the Devotion to the Seven Joys and Seven Dolours of St. Joseph.

One day, many, many years ago, there arose a terrible storm at sea. Many ships were wrecked off the coast of Flanders, and one of these was a large passenger vessel, with three hundred people on board.

Two Franciscan friars were among the number of the ill-fated crew, and when the final crash came, and the vessel went to pieces on the rocks, they retained sufficient presence of mind to keep together, and to clasp hold of a large plank as they fell into the water. Still, imagine their anguish, exposed on a cold night to all the fury of a raging sea, with nothing but a plank to rely on for safety. They felt their strength becoming exhausted, and they did not even know where they were, or how far from land.

In this extremity they devoutly invoked St. Joseph; and presently, with feelings of wonder and joy, the figure of a graceful-looking young man appeared suddenly standing beside them.

He saluted them most courteously, consoled them, and by his very presence seemed to impart to their chilled and stiffened limbs fresh vigour and strength. He did more, for he steered their frail plank so dextrously that it might have been a boat, and conducted them safely to the nearest point of land.

As soon as the good friars had safely landed they fell on their knees, and raising their hands and hearts to Almighty God, thanked Him for their wonderful preservation. Then they turned to their kind protector, and after the first fervent words of gratitude, one of them humbly said:

'Pray, good sir, who may you be, who have received such high gifts from God?'

And the young man answering said:

'I am Joseph, whom you called upon.'

On hearing these words, the souls of these devoted children of the blessed Francis overflowed with spiritual joy. They begged of their deliverer to tarry still a little longer with them, and he graciously consented, conversed with them concerning the sorrows and joys which he had experienced while living in this world; and he revealed to them that he would look down with pleasure from heaven on all who should venerate them, and piously meditate on them.

After he had thus spoken he disappeared.

This was the origin of the devotion to the seven joys and seven dolours of St. Joseph, now so widely spread throughout the Church, and enriched with so many indulgences.

11. S<small>AFETY IN</small> T<small>IME OF</small> D<small>ANGER</small>.

St. Theresa was travelling with some of her Religious to make one of her foundations, which she had promised to dedicate to St. Joseph. After a time, the coachman, unused to the country, lost his way and wandered from the road, if indeed the ill-defined track could be called a road; the horses became restive, and kept plunging about first on one side and then on another.

Suddenly St. Theresa saw herself and her daughters on the very brink of a dangerous precipice.

'My dear children,' she cried out, 'we are lost if our good father St. Joseph does not come to our rescue. Let us call on him for help.'

They had scarcely begun their prayer, when they heard a loud voice from the depths of the abyss calling out:

'Stop! Stop!'

At these words the horses immediately became quiet, and the same voice directed them concerning the path they were to take, hazardous enough certainly in appearance, yet they followed it with entire confidence, and soon all fear of danger was over.

The coachman and the whole company looked in vain to find the man who had rendered them such an important service. But they could not discover the slightest trace of him.

The Saint at first said nothing; her supernatural instinct had enabled her at once to grasp the real truth, and her heart was too full of gratitude for words; but at last, in reply to her companion's expressions of regret that they could not thank their benefactor, she replied:

'You seek in vain, my daughters, for the man who saved us.

It was no other than our dearest father, St. Joseph.'

12. UNDER THE PROTECTION OF ST. JOSEPH.

In the year 1631 a new and immense crater opened in Mount Vesuvius. Such a torrent of flames and ashes burst out that the glowing red lava, like a flood, covered the whole neighbourhood, especially a village called N——.

In this village lived a poor woman named Camilla, a most devout client of St. Joseph, and with her lived her little nephew, a child of about five years of age, named Joseph, out of devotion to her beloved patron.

When Camilla saw the streams of lava creeping down the sides of the mountain like fiery serpents, and gradually encircling all they met in their deadly embrace, she caught up the little boy in her arms and endeavoured to escape.

But alas! she had delayed too long. Fear seemed to lend her wings, and she flew rather than ran; but her cruel enemy pursued her ever faster and faster, gaining each moment on her. She did not see which way she was going; her one thought was to escape from the certain death following her so closely. Suddenly she found her path obstructed, she could go no further. Ah! poor woman, what have you done? In trying to escape one danger you have only encountered another nearly as formidable.

In her heedless aimless flight, she had directed her steps toward a high rock, which now rose perpendicularly before her, stretching away into the sea, so that it seemed impossible for her either to go backwards or forwards without losing her life. What could she do? If she turned back the flames would consume her; if she advanced it would be only to find certain death in the angry waves.

In this critical situation Camilla bethought herself of her holy patron.

'Great Saint,' she called out, 'I recommend to thee thy little Joseph, thou must save him.'

Having said these words she laid the child down on the rock, and herself ran down towards the sea. But instead of falling into the water, as it seemed she must naturally have done, she alighted on the sands, and did not suffer the slightest harm.

Herself saved, her next thought was for the little one, whom she had been forced to desert. The fate of the child, left to the mercy of the fire, grieved her exceedingly. In her sorrow and despair, she ran up and down, seeking him vainly everywhere.

All at once she heard his clear childish voice calling her by name, and better still, here he comes bounding to meet her full of life and joy.

'My sweetest one,' cried Camilla, 'who has saved thee from the fiery rain? who has rescued thee from being burned to death?'

'St. Joseph has done it, to whom thou didst entrust me;' replied the child. 'He took my hand and led me to that place where you found me.'

And instantly did this pious woman fall on her knees, most fervently thanking God and St. Joseph for the two miracles worked that day in her behalf.

O ye mothers, whose children often run into dangers a thousand times more perilous; redouble your prayers and your confidence in Our Blessed Lady and St. Joseph; redouble your care and your fervour in order to save the souls of your children.

13. Protection of St. Joseph during a Pestilence.

A terrible pestilence raged in Lyons during the year 1638. These scourges, as we well know, are often sent by God in His mercy to be a means of turning the hearts of His creatures to Himself, and in this affliction many were inspired to place themselves under the especial patronage of the glorious Foster-Father of Christ.

Their devotion was rewarded with the most signal graces, of which the following story is an instance.

A certain advocate was obliged to go to Lyons on business, and, as it seems to us, rather rashly, or perhaps forced by necessity, took with him his little son, who was only seven years old.

One day, being obliged to go out alone, on his return to the house, to his terror he found his child seized with the fatal malady and already in the agonies of death.

The unfortunate father, almost beside himself with grief, and despairing of human aid, turned himself to God, and besought Him through the intercession of St. Joseph to spare his son; making a promise at the same time to make a novena in honour of the Saint, to erect a votive tablet near his altar, and to offer a certain number of candles to burn before his statue.

Meanwhile the child kept each moment growing worse, and the doctor, declaring that it was impossible for him to live two hours longer, finally ordered him to be carried to the hospital, that the infection might not be increased.

The poor father followed the sad procession as mournfully as if he even now saw before him the little coffin of his son, yet his confidence in St. Joseph remained unshaken. And now listen how his faith was rewarded.

Hardly had they arrived at the hospital when the child suddenly sprang up from his bed, entirely restored to health, his rounded rosy features full of animation, and bearing no trace of his narrow escape from death.

Need we add that the grateful advocate hastened joyfully to fulfill his promises, and to glorify his heavenly Protector.

14. Protection of St. Joseph during a Contagious Disease.

Not many years ago, the following wonderful instance of an answer granted to prayer made a great sensation in the neighbourhood of Chambery.

It was the summer of 1861, and both the town itself and the whole country around were in a state of excitement and alarm, on account of a contagious disease which had appeared suddenly among the population, and the number of the victims continued to increase day by day.

The fervent parish priest of the Church of St. Pierre, seeing the danger and anguish of his flock, summoned them to the church, and exhorted them earnestly to place themselves under the special care of Mary and Joseph. He then organized a devotion for the next seven Sundays in honour of St. Joseph. On these occasions the church was filled to overflowing, and numberless candles were presented at the altar of the Saint.

The compassionate Heart of our Divine Lord showed itself merciful to these humble supplications offered to Him through the intervention of His Immaculate Mother and chaste Foster-

Father. For although the disease raged in the other parts of the town, for full three months longer, not one more fatal case occurred in this parish; and while the bells of the neighbouring churches were continually tolling the sad announcement of death, the bells of St. Pierre were only heard from time to time on festival days or sounding the glad news of some baptism or marriage.

Devotion to St. Joseph, which already had taken deep root in the heart of these faithful Catholics, became more lively, and in all their affairs they had recourse with unbounded confidence to the intercession of Mary and Joseph.

15. St. Joseph all-powerful with God.

The 8th of September, 1860, was a sad day in the home of a respectable family living in a certain town in Poland, for it saw the husband and father of the family deprived, by political intrigues, of a situation which he had filled well and conscientiously.

It is true, it was not a very lucrative employment; yet it was their only means of support; besides enabling the parents to give their children a good education. Now, all was gone, and they knew not how to procure the most necessary means of subsistence.

The anxiety and sudden change from a life of comparative comfort to one of want and misery were too much for poor Madame N——and she fell into a kind of nervous excitement, accompanied with fever, and great prostration. Her friends endeavoured to calm her, and raise her spirits, but all in vain, as she easily perceived that their kind words were only spoken from charity, and to give her a confidence which they did not themselves share.

She grew daily worse, until her old father, who was very devoted to St. Joseph, and who was much grieved to see her in this state, became inspired as to the right method of offering her relief.

Entering her room one morning quite cheerfully, he said to her:

'Well, my dear daughter, what are you doing? are you going to allow yourself to become quite a prey to these "blue-devils!" '

'But, my father,' she replied, 'how can you joke at our misery?'

'Yes, my daughter,' returned the old man, 'I am not troubled about it, for I have put it into the hands of St. Joseph, and I am sure his loving heart will never forsake us. I assure you that I have never asked any favour of him which I did not receive; therefore, courage, my child, do you also ask him for help, and your prayer will be heard.'

The afflicted daughter followed the advice of her father, and invoked the great Saint, yet more by her tears than by her words.

And who would believe it? Scarcely had she finished her short but devout prayer, when she felt interiorly so calm and peaceful, it was like passing again from death to life. In less than two hours she had regained her former strength, and with renewed health and vigour was able to resume her ordinary household duties.

Those who had seen her, only a few hours before, wasting away on a sick bed, dull and miserable, could hardly believe their eyes; and St. Joseph, apparently not satisfied even with this, took care to send her husband some good friends who assisted them in their poverty.

A long time after, Madame N——received a letter from her brother, who was also now in great distress. His wife had fallen dangerously ill, and her life was despaired of by the doctor. Therefore, her husband wrote to beg his sister to come and assist her, and also to be a comfort to him when the sad moment should come of separation from his much-loved wife.

Madame N——at once set off on her journey; and, on arriving at her destination was met by her brother, whom she found full of sorrow, and quite despairing of the recovery of his wife.

'Have you invoked St. Joseph?' asked Madame N——.

'Yes,' he replied, 'ever since my wife was declared to be in danger, I have burned a lamp before his statue, and I have often invoked him; but I do not think myself worthy of so great a favour.'

Let us now listen to Madame N——'s own narration.

'When the evening came, I retired to take a little rest, as I was fatigued with my long journey, and depressed by the sight of my brother's great affliction; but before we parted, we once again, fervently and with confidence, besought St. Joseph on behalf of the poor sufferer.

'I had gone to sleep, when suddenly I was awakened by hearing my name called. I rose hastily, and prepared to return to the sick room, thinking that the last moment had arrived, and that I was wanted. But, no! it was, instead, the moment of help from St. Joseph. A crisis of the disease had indeed come, but, contrary to all hope, it was favourable. She, whom we had thought dying, now slept quietly and soundly, and when the doctor came the next morning to visit his patient, to his intense astonishment, he found her so far recovered that he declared it could only have happened through a miracle.'

In a very short time her health was completely restored, so that no trace of her former illness remained.

16. S<small>PEEDY</small> H<small>ELP</small>.

A very pious, but poor woman, was in distress for five shillings to complete the payment of her rent, which was due on Christmas Day. The sum was small; but still she knew not how to procure it. In her distress she applied with great confidence to St. Joseph, and placed her difficulty in his hands.

After doing this, she left her house on some business. As she returned, a letter was handed to her; but, behold, inside there were five shillings, just the sum she needed. She had not the slightest idea from whom it came.

17. A W<small>ONDERFUL</small> C<small>URE</small>.

A poor widow, named Wilhelmina Rielz, who lived at Newbau, in Vienna, fell dangerously ill of a most painful disease: and being confined to her bed, was unable to work to support her four little children.

By the influence of some charitable persons, she was taken to the hospital of the Franciscan nuns, in Hartsmann Street, Vienna, where the doctors decided she must undergo a very serious and painful operation, as a large and deep ulcer had formed on the head, behind the ear. The incisions made were very deep, and the daily dressing of the wound was so painful, that the poor woman often fainted under it. At last, the physician declared that disease had affected the bone, and gave very little hope of cure, saying that her sufferings would last a long time.

In this sad situation, rendered even more painful to the poor mother by the anxiety concerning her little children, for whose subsistence she was unable to labour, she turned herself with great fervour to her holy Patron, St. Joseph, to whom she had ever been most devoted, and she desired to receive the Sacraments with this intention. After receiving Holy Communion on the following morning, she fell, as it were, into a kind of slumber; it seemed to her as if the great Patriarch appeared standing at her bedside, and her soul became filled with consolation and confidence.

Wilhelmina knew not whether it was a dream or a reality; but she felt so great a peace, and such full certainty that she should recover, that she could not doubt that it was a great grace received from God, and, indeed, the wound which was three inches deep, in three days was perfectly healed.

The physician was amazed, and declared he had never in all his practice experienced such a cure before.

The good sisters and invalids in the hospital were not less surprised at this visible supernatural cure, and all united in thanking God for His goodness.

In a few days, after the physicians had once more carefully examined the wound, the happy widow left the hospital (on the 16th of March, 1885), and since then has continued well, and in good health. Not even a scar of the fearful ulcer and wound remain.

This is again proof of St. Joseph's readiness to assist the faithful, when they devoutly call on him for help.

To everyone we say with confidence: 'Go to Joseph.' The great Saint will grant each humble petition, if it is for the honour of God and the good of the suppliant.

18. SHELTER AT MIDNIGHT.

Last year, whilst I was at Minden, in Westphalia, writes P. D. of Paderborn, Sister Michael, the Superioress of the Franciscans (a branch from Aix-la-Chapelle), related to me the following:

Two of their sisters, who were in one of their convents in North America, were sent to a distant town, where the Bishop of the diocese resided, and where he wished to make a foundation.

They had to travel a day and a half and one night, so that they reached the place just at midnight. They were greatly distressed at arriving at so inconvenient an hour—strangers in a strange place, they knew not what to do. Thus they thought to themselves, as the train brought them nearer and nearer to their destination. Then one of them, turning to the other, said:

'I can think of nothing better than to recommend ourselves to the care and protection of St. Joseph.

This they did at once, invoking most fervently and earnestly the great Patriarch's help and assistance.

It was midnight; the train stopped at a large station. The sisters got out and stood bewildered and helpless, uncertain what to do. But, they had not to wait long, for a coachman approaching them civilly, asked them to get into the carriage which was waiting for them; when they questioned him, with astonishment, as to what or whose carriage was waiting, he said that the Bishop had sent him to meet them, and to let them know rooms were already prepared for them. And so it was they found all arranged as if they had been expected that night.

The next morning, when the sisters met the Bishop, they explained to him their anxiety and perplexity at the station, and thanked him for his kindness in sending the carriage, and for his hospitality.

But the Bishop was amazed; for he knew nothing whatever about it, nor had he given any orders concerning the nuns.

Who, then, could have done it? Who sent the carriage? May we not believe it was St. Joseph, whom they had so trustingly invoked?

19. Protection in Danger from Fire.

'On the 10th of December, 1879, a fire broke out in our village in the house of a Jew. The cause was unknown, but as the house was thatched, the fire spread quickly, and before help could be obtained the whole roof was one mass of flames.

'The fire was very near my presbytery; at the first alarm I awoke, and seeing the danger, prostrated before my oratory and besought the protection of God, through the intercession of our great patron St. Joseph. My prayer was not in vain; very soon the hand of God became visible, for although the burning house was entirely in flames before help arrived, and although the next house, which was only four yards distant, was also thatched with straw, the fire remained limited to the first house only, and a wind rising just at the time drove the flames in a direction where there were no buildings.

'The same night I was enlightened by God to understand better the wonderful effects of the intercession of the Saints. As soon as the danger was over I went back to bed, fell asleep, and dreamed that I was hastening again to the scene of the fire, desirous of doing all in my power to extinguish the flames. As

I drew near to the spot, I met a procession of girls dressed in white, who carried the statue of St. Anthony of Padua. Close behind this procession followed another, bearing statues of Our Blessed Lady and St. Joseph, and carrying lighted candles in their hands. They all went forward until they came close to the fire, when they put down their statues on the ground, knelt down and prayed.

'The flames appeared obstinate, they came forward, and even licked round about the statue of St. Anthony, but they could not enkindle it, and gradually seemed to be becoming extinguished. Just at this moment the ringing of the bells awoke me, and so my dream ended.

'Two years ago I had another experience of a fire suddenly extinguished by the intercession of St. Joseph.

'We have a Confraternity of St. Joseph established in this parish, which is continually increasing in numbers, as it is a belief among my parishioners that no one who joins it will die without the grace of the last Sacraments.'

20. St. Joseph saves a Child from Death by Fire.

In affliction, tribulation, danger, temptation, family troubles—indeed, in every want both spiritual and temporal—St. Joseph has always and everywhere been a protector.

Now listen how wonderfully a child in the Tyrol escaped being burned to death. It happened thus:

Fire had broken out in a certain house, and almost before the inhabitants could be roused, the whole building was enveloped in flames.

In the terror and confusion which ensued, it happened that a woman had got separated from her child, and dragged out almost before she knew where she was. When she recognised that she was safe, and her little one left behind in peril, the anguish of the poor mother was terrible to behold. She threw herself on her knees, and entreated the bystanders to save her child. But although all shared her sorrow, it was impossible to enter amidst the raging flames.

Then the unhappy woman, seeing that all human aid failed her, besought heavenly succour. Raising her eyes and hands to heaven, she invoked St. Joseph, saying:

'Hail, Joseph, to thee I recommend my Joseph, my only child!'

And miraculously the fire seemed to divide on either side of the little room where lay the cradle of the sleeping infant, and the mother's heart was rejoiced once again, by clasping in her arms the treasure she feared that she had lost. Thanks to St. Joseph.

21. DELIVERANCE FROM ROBBERS.

Some years ago the whole country near — — was made unsafe by a notorious highwayman. One day he attacked a burgomaster on his way from his receiving-office, and having taken from him a large sum of money, left him lying insensible on the road.

Some people passing soon afterwards found him still alive, and when he somewhat recovered, he was able to give an exact description of the bandit, which was inserted in the local newspapers.

Among the many who read this paragraph was a certain poor young girl, who on the very next day was obliged on account of some needlework to walk a long way to the house of the head-forester of the district. In vain she attempted to find some escort or protection—no one seemed to be going in that direction; so she had to set out alone, trusting in God's assistance, and, according to her custom, saying her Rosary as she went along. Her road led her directly through the forest, where the brigand was known to lie concealed; and often did the girl turn her eyes in the direction where she knew stood the Church of——, containing a beautiful chapel dedicated to St. Joseph, as if to seek from him the protection she so much needed.

She had already advanced about half-way through the forest; and she was intending to rest for a few minutes on a little bench placed near the road-side for travellers, and which commanded an opening through the trees and a lovely view of the St.——Lake, with its blue waters glittering and dancing in the morning sunshine. Suddenly she became paralysed with terror, for she saw a man emerge from behind a tree, and recognised in him, from the description which she had read, the very person she feared to meet. They met face to face; he measured her with cruel, greedy looks, and seemed to enjoy her evident agony of fear.

Help seemed impossible in such a lonely spot, and at such an early hour.

'Hail, Joseph, is there no hope of deliverance for me?'

This was all she could articulate with her trembling lips. But, oh wonder! at this very moment, the voices of two youths were heard, and she saw them coming along talking gaily together.

As they passed the maiden, they saluted her courteously, but passed on quickly without stopping. She, on her part, followed them instantly, and the robber also came on, but more slowly, not daring to attack her in such company. After some time they came to an open space, where several men were at work felling trees. Then the highwayman in his turn, being afraid, slunk back into the depths of the forest, and was seen no more.

The two youths seemed suddenly to disappear; the men who were working could find no trace of them, and, notwithstanding many eager inquiries from the girl, both at the forester's house, and in all the neighbourhood, no one could tell her who they were, or had even seen them. She described them as being both dressed alike, with such sweet and pleasant faces as she had never seen before.

The village girl never relates this story without many grateful tears for the kind protection sent her by her beloved St. Joseph.

22. An Engineer.

From the Ardennes, an engineer sends us an account of his escape from a sudden death.

He was engaged in some difficult work, and every day it was his custom to visit a chapel of the glorious Patriarch, to beg of him protection and safety for soul and body, and, also, on all occasions he openly professed himself a client of St. Joseph.

The Saint richly rewarded his fidelity; for one night, just as he had entered on his duties, and was mounting up on the engine, the steam boiler burst; six men were killed, and others more or less severely wounded, while he, who might have expected instant death, was preserved unhurt.

In thanksgiving for this signal deliverance, he at once had the Holy Sacrifice of the Mass offered in honour of St. Joseph, and himself received Holy Communion seven times.

23. A Small Gift Towards Building a Church in Honour of St. Joseph Recompensed a Hundredfold.

A young man once came to the parish-priest of a town in Westphalia, who was building a church in honour of St. Joseph, and offered him a small contribution. In the course of the conversation which ensued, the priest learnt that the young man was in great pecuniary difficulties, and that the small sum he had just given for the church was the last piece of money he possessed in the world. Yet he had sacrificed it joyfully, trusting that the blessed Foster-Father of Jesus would deliver him from his trouble. Deeply moved by such firm faith and confidence, the priest could hardly control his tears sufficiently to thank him.

Some months passed away, and, fully engrossed in his undertaking, the pastor of N——had nearly forgotten the occurrence, when one morning a letter arrived, bearing the post-mark of a distant town in Germany, and directed in an unknown hand. As he opened the envelope several bank-notes of considerable value fell out, and a letter from the same young man, stating that he had been wonderfully rescued from all his difficulties, and therefore, sent the enclosed money as a thanksgiving offering to St. Joseph, begging the priest to use it for the adornment of his church.

24. LITTLE JOSEPH DE MALINCKROOT.

It may please our readers, especially those who are acquainted with Germany, to hear something about the little child of a man highly esteemed in that country.

The account was sent to the German editor of these stories by a friend. He writes as follows:

'Lately two Franciscan nuns from the mother-house at Aix-la-Chapelle were here to collect alms. One of them, a Countess Stolberg, told us that about a year ago they were sent to Berlin for the same purpose.'

We will now let the Religious speak for herself:

'At Berlin, Madame de Malinckroot constituted herself our especial hostess in the most generous, self-sacrificing manner. She accompanied us everywhere, and rendered us the greatest service.

'On day, late in the afternoon, she took us to the house of Herr Borsig (engine manufacturer). We asked to see Madame Borsig, who soon appeared, but received us coldly and indifferently, and even appeared, as I though, somewhat annoyed.

'Whilst I was making my appeal, she was called away, and asked us to await her return; but she was so long absent, that I began to be quite uncomfortable that Madame de Malinckroot should be so inconveniently detained; and, perhaps, even at home, her husband might also be waiting for her. In my distress, I said to myself, not thinking to be overheard:

' "St. Joseph, please help us that we may receive something."

'But my words reached the sharp ears of Madame de Malinckroot's little son, who was with us (and who, as his name was Joseph, was taught to have great devotion to his

Patron Saint). His mother then said to him:

' "Joseph, say a little prayer to your Patron Saint, that these good sisters may receive some money for their poor; tell him to make Madame Borsig give them one hundred dollars (£15)."

'The little fellow looked all around the room for a picture of St. Joseph, and not finding one, he contented himself with saying an "Our Father," that his petition might be granted.

Shortly afterwards Madame Borsig returned, and at once, presented me with one hundred dollars. Then the child said innocently to the lady:

' "We all said a prayer that you might give us something, and so you have done it."

'When he returned home, he repeated the story to his father, and, indeed, we could not but consider it remarkable that Madame Borsig, who apparently had taken very little interest in us, should give us the largest sum of money which we received from anyone in Germany.

'May the dear little Joseph always remain worthy of his heavenly Patron.

'Some time previously, he had said to his mother one day, when he saw a nice cake on the table:

' "Mother, please give me a big slice of that cake for the parish priest."

'And when she asked: "Why?" he replied:

' "Because he preached this morning about St. Joseph." '

25. A True Story of the Franco-Prussian War.

On the 28th of February, 1871, the Very Rev. Canon Victor Pelletier, of the diocese of Orleans, at the close of one of his Lenten discourses, announced to his auditors that the month of

St. Joseph would begin on the following day. He gave them some reasons to encourage them to share in this devotion, and reminded them of the decree, then lately published by Pius IX., raising the feast of St. Joseph to a festival of the highest rank for the universal Church, and then he related to them the following occurrence.

On Sunday, the 14th of December, 1870, the Prussians forced their way for the second and third time into the little town of Patay, a few miles distant from Orleans.

The Zouaves offered an heroic resistance, but were overpowered by numbers, and forced to retire with great loss. Just as the French troops were retreating, Madame L——the wife of a merchant in the town, who had the charge of her husband's business, remembered that there was still a large sum of money in the house.

Calling for two or three of her confidential servants, they consulted together, and finally resolved to conceal the money in a well close to the house. There was no time to be lost, so at once they set out; the lady herself descended first into the well, and the others followed her, each carrying a part of the money. While they were still down below, they heard a loud stamping overhead, then a rough shout which terrified them; but they whispered to each other to keep quite quiet, and hoped that the increasing darkness might favour their escape from discovery.

But in vain! Almighty God did not intend to preserve them in this way. A Prussian soldier had forced his way into the house, and finding no one within, had come out to search the garden. He soon perceived the well uncovered, and felt sure that the inhabitants were hidden there. He called down several times into the darkness, for he could not see to the bottom, and when he received no answer he threatened to throw in combustibles and set them on fire. The Prussian, as the French well knew, was quite capable of carrying his design into execution, so poor Madame L——and her servants were obliged to answer, and then to trust themselves to the mercy of their enemy.

They clambered out again as best they could, Madame L——courageously leading the way, and carrying the bag which contained the greater part of the money. The quick eye of the Prussian at once noticed the bag.

'What are you hiding there?' he demanded.

The poor lady thought it wiser to make her sacrifice without difficulty, so, emptying the money on the ground, she replied:

'You are the master, take what you like.

'I am a soldier, not a thief,' retorted the man. 'Put up your money, and come back quietly to the house.'

Madame L——and her servants obeyed with pleasure, for this declaration on the part of the foe was quite unexpected. And, indeed, he seemed more a friend than an enemy, for all the rest of that night he remained as a sentinel outside the house, thus preserving it from being plundered by any of the other Prussian soldiers.

But how was this kindness and disinterestedness to be explained? Here is the answer.

Madame L——was a good Christian, and at the first announcement of danger she had placed herself, her house and her possessions under the protection of St. Joseph, and he, as we have seen, did not fail his client in the time of difficulty and distress.

26. ST. JOSEPH ANSWERS THE PRAYER OF A CHILD.

The midnight hour had already passed, and all around was quiet and still. But in one of the poorest huts of a village in the south of Italy the deep silence was broken by cries and sobs, which came from the overloaded heart of a poor peasant girl, Agnes, as she was called.

She was kneeling by the bedside of her father, who appeared to be in his last agony. Only half an hour before, the priest had given him all the last Sacraments and blessings of holy Church, to prepare and strengthen him for his passage into another world. And now he was struggling with death. His weeping child supported him as best she could in her arms. She had never known her mother, who died when she was only an infant; and he whom she was now losing had been father, mother, and all to her. Her tears fell fast over his face and breast, but the dying man did not see or feel them.

One kind woman from a neighbouring cottage, with that unfailing charity of the poor for each other, which seems equally a characteristic of all nations and countries, was passing the night in a corner of the room, in case she might be any use or comfort to Agnes, and she spent her time in telling her beads for the soul which seemed hovering on the threshold of the other world.

Suddenly about daybreak the bells of the village church began to ring.

'What is that for?' asked Agnes.

'Do you not remember,' replied the woman, 'that to-day is the feast of St. Joseph?'

'O blessed St. Joseph!' cried the child, and fell on her knees; 'O dear St. Joseph, help! *Thou* must help me! Save my father!'

And at the same moment she felt inspired with such a great confidence in the powerful assistance of St. Joseph, that she firmly depended on his help. Then she quickly rose, put her mouth to the ear of her father, and said to him:

'Father, you will not yet die; St. Joseph will help you.'

And strange to tell, the dying man slowly recovered his senses, opened his eyes, and gradually became better and better, although still weak and suffering, for it pleased Almighty God only to restore his health by degrees.

But hope in the intercession of St. Joseph ever animated him, and on the day the bells rang again to usher in the sweet month of Mary, among the crowd of devout peasants who hastened to do homage to the blessed Mother of God were Agnes and her father.

And no more loving and grateful prayers ascended that day before the throne of God than came from these two simple hearts, once so sorrowful, now so grateful and glad.

27. Two true Stories from Westphalia.

I.

This little anecdote may seem trifling to some readers, but we have not hesitated to insert it, to show that the same Divine Providence which clothes the lilies of the field in beauty, not equalled by all the glory of Solomon, will no despise the needs of the poor when they cry for help; and that Christ will take, if we may venture to use the expression, extra delight in relieving their necessities, through the medium of His Foster-Father.

One summer, on account of the long-continued and heavy rains, the harvest was later than usual. My husband, who was already advanced in years, sought in vain for some assistance, and at last became quite discouraged. Long before, we had dedicated our house and farm and all our possessions to St. Joseph, and one day the words of St. Teresa came into my mind, 'that she never asked St. Joseph anything without being heard;' so I knelt down, and said to St. Joseph with the greatest confidence, and quite like a child:

'Blessed Saint, you are the patron and father of our family; do now your duty and procure us help.'

Quite comforted by my prayer, I then rose, as the answer seemed sure to me, and quite calmly threw myself into the bosom of Divine Providence, waiting for the moment of help to come, although I could not imagine how God would answer me.

Two days after, a strong youth came to the house and asked for something to eat; I gave it to him, and asked if he understood field-work. He answered in a vague manner, and continued his meal. The next day he proceeded on his journey during a heavy shower, but scarcely had he been absent from us for half-an-hour, before he felt an interior voice which said to him again and again, 'Go back to those people.' This he himself has told me since, and I need only add that we have never had a better aid.

II.

A family well-known to me had been quite ruined by misfortune.

The poor people, already advanced in years felt themselves

forsaken by God and man. The thought that they were losing all their possessions, and becoming quite destitute, caused them the greatest grief of heart.

In this their distress, they addressed themselves to St. Joseph, and laid all their needs and tribulations before him, and especially they made many novenas in his honour, that he might inspire them what to do.

A friend one day recommended them to engage some young man as bailiff, who understood the management of a farm like theirs, and as his advice seemed good, they determined to follow it.

Several offers were made in answer to their inquiries, and they immediately began a fresh novena, that they might make a right choice. On the ninth day they received a letter from a young person who seemed to possess all the qualifications they were seeking, and being persuaded that he was sent in answer to their prayer, they engaged him; and truly St. Joseph did not disappoint them, for no son could have served them more devotedly, or taken greater care of their interests than did this young man; through whose endeavours their property was soon rescued from ruin, and the declining years of this good couple made peaceful and happy.

28. A Letter to St. Joseph.

Towards the end of the seventeenth century the suburb of Vienna called 'Laimgrube,' did not consist of the splendid buildings to be seen there at the present day; there were some handsome mansions belonging to the wealthy citizens, but by far the greater part consisted of miserable little houses, into one of which we must beg our kind reader to enter.

It stood in Maria Helfer street, a miserable tumbledown-looking old place, and if we enter without knocking, after the manner of Angels or story-tellers, and go up the rickety staircase into the worst room of this dilapidated house, we shall find it to be tenanted by the gifted musician Paul Merten and his daughter Josepha, only sixteen years of age, beautiful and well educated, and especially accomplished in all kinds of embroidery and needlework.

But just at the time when our story begins misery and want were rife in Vienna. Very few years had elapsed since it had been besieged by the savage Turks, and although they had been successfully repulsed, yet war always leaves poverty and suffering in its train, and the inhabitants of Vienna had hardly as yet either the inclination or the means of enjoying unnecessary luxuries.

But the superfluities of the rich often constitute the necessary means of subsistence of the poor, and so it was in the present case; because not one could afford to take music lessons, or give orders for ornamental needlework, poor Paul Merten and his daughter often had to go to bed cold and hungry.

One day, when their distress seemed to have reached its height, Josepha could no longer bear to see her father suffering and complaining.

'Father,' she said, 'I shall go and seek a situation as a servant, then at least I can send you my wages.'

'What!' cried the old man, 'will you also leave me? who then shall I have to wait upon me? by no means, I will never allow it.'

'But, dear father,' replied Josepha, 'at present, I have no other way to help you at all; you know I wrote long ago to the husband of my late godmother, as our last chance of assistance, and I have not as yet had any answer at all.'

'No wonder,' excitedly returned the old man, 'you might as well have written to the devil.' For he was wild with grief and hunger, and did not quite know what he was saying.

'Fie, father! What bad thoughts misery puts in your mind,' cried the child. 'Let us rather address ourselves to my dear Patron Saint, that he may obtain for us from Our Lord help and employment.'

'Do you mean to say,' retorted her father bitterly, 'that you really believe that the poor carpenter has such great credit in heaven? Well, write to St. Joseph if you like, and much good may it do you.'

'Father, that is indeed a good idea, which I will carry out immediately,' replied cheerfully the devout little Josepha; 'I will write to him, and my white dove, to which I cannot to-day give even a crumb of bread, shall be my little carrier.'

She sat down at her father's desk, and on a little piece of paper she wrote the following words:

'Hail, Joseph! have mercy on us in our great distress. We have no work, no subsistence; ask our dear Lord to send me some employment, for my father is suffering from hunger.

'Thy faithful namesake,
'JOSEFA MERTEN,
'Needlewoman, and daughter
of the musician.

'Laimgrube, in Maria Helfer Street, No. 13.'

She folded up her note, tied it round the neck of the dove by a silken thread, opened the window, and the little thin dove fluttered slowly away.

An hour had hardly passed, when there sounded a loud knock at the door. Old Paul Merten called out 'Come in,' and a stately handsome gentleman entered the miserable apartment.

'Does the honourable Fraulein Merten live here? he inquired.

'Yes,' replied the father shortly, and casting rather a distrustful look at the stranger. 'What do you want with her?'

'My name is Joseph Charles Hirte, and I am a jeweller in the city,' he answered kindly. 'I live in this neighbourhood, and I have received a message from St. Joseph, to whom I am very devout, to answer in his name the letter written to him by your daughter. I want a great deal of work done, and your daughter must execute it nicely for me. I have also enrolled myself as a member in the choir of the Carmelite Church, and I need some lessons to make me more perfect. Will you and your daughter undertake the task?'

'O yes, with the greatest of pleasure,' cried Josepha with glistening eyes.

'Well,' continued Herr Hirte, 'you must allow me to pay a certain sum in advance, as this is my invariable rule in all business transactions.'

So saying, he laid five shining ducats on the table.

'O father!' cried the girl, 'do you not see how favourably St. Joseph has received my letter?—how fervently I shall thank him!'

'Yes, Fraulein, do that always, and surely you will not remain without consolation and help,' said the citizen gravely and earnestly. 'I will send you all necessary materials for your work by my servant, and hope soon to hear from you. And you sir,' he added, turning to Paul Merten, 'will you kindly come to-morrow to begin my lessons? Here is my address; you cannot fail to find the house, as outside is painted a large picture of St. Joseph.' He then saluted them respectfully and departed.

The daughter threw herself into her father's arms, shedding tears of joy; but he cast his eyes down in shame and repentance.

And now how simple was the solution of this affair, effected by the watchful care of Divine Providence.

The little dove, weak with hunger and frightened and fatigued by its unaccustomed burden, was not able to fly far, but had sought refuge near at hand. Chance, or rather we should say the design of God, had made it alight at the open window of the room where Herr Hirte was sitting, who was much surprised to see his unexpected guest, and to perceive the tiny note suspended round its neck.

He untied it, and read it; and moved by the pious confidence of this child, had resolved at once to reward it.

But we must not conclude without giving quite the end of our story. After some time, the rich merchant, seeing and admiring the many good qualities of Josepha, asked her in marriage of her father, who willingly accepted the proposal of their generous benefactor; and so it came to pass that the poor Josepha Merten became the honourable and wealthy Madame Hirte, who, as a sign of her gratitude to St. Joseph, had a beautiful representation made of the Saint, and placed as a shield on the little house where once she had lived in poverty and sorrow, and until this day the shield may still be seen there.

29. A Good Situation Obtained.

To-day we must take a long journey and go far, far away, until we reach Perth, the capital of Queensland, in Australia.

There was once living there an Irishman, of course a Catholic, and, nearly as much a matter of course, the father of a large family. He toiled day and night at work of the hardest and most fatiguing description to procure the necessary means of subsistence for his numerous family. Yet still the poor mother, with an aching heart, was often compelled to send her little ones supperless to bed.

Each trial made by the good man to better his condition had ended in total failure; and so years passed on: the children were growing older, and still the family remained in the same squalid poverty. The mother suffered most of all; anxiety was wearing and fretting away her very life, her loving but ineffectual solicitude for her hard-working husband, and her boys and girls pale from want of nourishing food, and ignorant from the impossibility of procuring education.

One evening, when both parents were particularly harassed on account of some trifling debt, which they were unable to discharge, a neighbour, passing by, lent them a newspaper, and the man's eye chanced to fall the first thing on an announcement that a certain situation had become vacant, which was in the disposal of the Government of the colony.

It was a lucrative post, and one in every way suited to his wishes and capabilities. But how could he, poor and unknown, moreover a Catholic and an Irishman, compete for such a position in a place crowded with bigoted Protestants and professed Freemasons? All these difficulties he was only too well aware of, and yet the bitter poverty of his home, and the firm confidence of his wife, inspired him with a courageous resolution.

'Dear wife,' he said, 'humanly speaking, I have not the slightest chance of obtaining this desirable situation, which would be the making of our fortune; but with confidence in the blessed St. Joseph, I will nevertheless make the attempt. I will go to the place and make personal efforts to obtain what I want. In the meantime, you and the children must pray that St. Joseph may bless my endeavours.'

No sooner said than acted upon. The good man, as may be imagined, did not require long to make his preparations, and set off early the next morning, while Pat and Mike, Steve and Barney, Molly and Biddy, were roused from their sleep by their mother, with the good news that father had gone to get them plenty of money and food, and that if they would only pray hard to St. Joseph, they would never be hungry nor ragged any more. And so these little Catholic children, with that unhesitating faith which belongs to their religion alone, knelt down around their devout mother and began a Novena of nine Aves for father's success.

How could the tender mercy of God Who calls Himself the 'Father of the poor' be insensible to the petitions offered Him from these innocent childish hearts?

It was the ninth and last day of the Novena when about half past nine in the evening a hasty knock was heard at the cottage-door, and a man thrust in one of those brownish yellow papers known so well to us all under the name of 'Telegram.'

The poor woman's heart gave one great bound as she took it from the hand of the messenger. Was it to be the bearer of sorrow or joy?

She opened it; yes, joy! thank God! her husband had been

accepted.

A few tears of the most ardent gratitude fell from her eyes; and then she sought her children, and made them rise at once and kneel down with her to return thanks to God.

Now this family lives in ease and affluence, and the future fortunes of the children seem secure.

In the town itself the news caused the most boundless astonishment. How came this poor and unknown stranger to obtain such a brilliant position, whilst the best applications had been refused?

One day when the Bishop of the Diocese asked the two parents who had been the powerful friends whose influence had secured them such an excellent situation, they gave this true and beautiful answer:

'No one here below, but one who is more powerful and kind than all the friends on earth—St. Joseph; to him we owe all our fortune.'

30. THE ROLL OF MONEY.

In the year 1864, so writes a priest from Russia, I began the construction of the church in B——. My money failing, I had recourse to the intercession of St. Joseph, and asked some rich Protestant families for a contribution. The first immediately gave £15. On my way home I wished to bring my collection to the builder, but, absorbed in my anxieties, I went, contrary to my intention, into his neighbour's house. In the centre of the otherwise empty table of the sitting-room lay a roll of money.

I related to the master of the house what, through the intercession of St. Joseph, I had collected from some Protestant families for the building of the church. The tears came into his eyes:

'Take then,' said he, 'this roll of money also, for my name is Joseph.'

31. St. Joseph Helps to Build Churches and Schools.

Another priest writes:

My present mission was only newly-established; I desired much to open the poor school in October, but there were no desks, no blackboard, no stone, and not a penny was at my disposal. I began a Novena to Jesus, Mary and Joseph, and said only a few 'Our Fathers.' Some days afterwards, in the waiting-room of the station, a lady addressed me. I related to her my troubles. As she was getting into the train, she put a paper into my hand of twenty-five florins. That was the first visible help, and from thenceforth St. Joseph has assisted me in all my troubles, which have not been few. I had nothing; he has supplied all. It is true, I wrote numberless letters, but he disposed the hearts. I do not know where the money came from. The greater part always came in the month of March, though once in January he sent me 400 dollars.

Now and then St. Joseph seemed to delay, and then I would humbly admonish him. The presbytery and little church are finished, and St. Joseph has paid all my debts.

32. St. Joseph in the Oak.

In the month of May, 1856, by the desire of the parish priest, a Mission was given in Villedieu, in the diocese of Angers, by

Father Louis, a priest of the Society of Jesus. At the end of it, the parish priest took him to see an extraordinarily old oak tree, which was one of the curiosities of the place. Whilst Father Louis was occupied measuring the circumference of this giant oak, which was no less than twenty yards, the thought struck him to place a statue of St. Joseph in the large hole which the lapse of centuries had formed in its trunk by reason of the great age of this huge tree; which at the present moment was only utilized as a shelter for protection against the weather, and which might easily be converted into a little chapel. The parish priest readily agreed to this proposal, and so did the family to whom the oak belonged, and the ecclesiastical authorities.

Soon an altar with a tabernacle was erected, and a statue of St. Joseph was likewise placed in it, and the first time that Holy Mass was offered there, the holy Spouse of the Immaculate Mother of God was invoked under the title of 'St. Joseph in the Oak.' This title was universally recognised with great rejoicing by one hundred priests and fifteen hundred laity who were present on the occasion, and has belonged to the pilgrimage ever since.

The tidings of this inauguration re-echoed throughout the whole land, and from thenceforth, the Holy Sacrifice of the Mass was continually offered up in this new sanctuary. More than thirty thousand pilgrims flocked from all parts, and associated themselves with the inhabitants of Villedieu to praise the Saint, and to implore his powerful intercession in their troubles and anxieties, who had become their especial patron and protector. Dating from this day, there has ascended an unceasing universal homage from this modest sanctuary to the exalted Patriarch, which in the last twenty years has steadily increased. And Heaven has responded to the homage of the pilgrims by the most remarkable graces, which show how agreeable to God are their praises, their petitions, and their pious promises in this holy place.

The Holy Father, by a brief of the 23rd of June, 1857, endowed and enriched this pilgrimage with indulgences. This favour contributed not a little to raise it to greater importance among the faithful of the district, and very soon it was indispensably necessary to build a chapel to enable the many pilgrims to satisfy their devotion. The money for its accomplishment was altogether wanting; but the generosity of the clients of St. Joseph, of the inhabitants, and of the pilgrims themselves, supplied the means. Nor was it very long before this also did not suffice. So now there stands a church at the foot of the old oak, worthy of its destination. With what faith, with what confidence, and with what lively interest one feels drawn to this sanctuary cannot be expressed. Pilgrimages are made to it from Anjou, Bretagne, and Poitou; and even from the northern and distant provinces of Belgium, and other quarters, come pilgrimages and processions. These arrive every year—from sixty to eighty thousand pilgrims; and over seven hundred Masses are said at the place of pilgrimage itself. Not a day passes without bringing some new pilgrims, but the greatest number arrive at the time of the principal feast in the month of August.

Then all those who have obtained hearing and help from St. Joseph, likewise those who have fresh graces to ask him, come on these festival days to join in the solemnities and homage which there take place in honour of the holy Patriarch, and not unfrequently does his power manifest itself by new and wonderful benefits.

A young priest had edified us very much during the ceremonies of the High Mass of the feast. He performed the function of Deacon with extraordinary piety. After the Mass, he approached the priest of the Mission, who, with the parish priest of Villedieu, had founded this sanctuary.

'Do you recognise me, Father?' he asked.

'No; I do not know that I have ever met you.'

'What! you do not know me?' said the young priest. 'Look here,' and he showed him a large, deep scar on his hand.

'What! is it you?' exclaimed the priest; 'how glad and happy I am to see you again. The prayer of your excellent mother in that desperate case was then heard. St. Joseph be praised.'

What had happened to him? To the greater honour and glory of St. Joseph, we will willingly relate it to our readers.

In the winter of the year 1858, a little boy of seven years old accompanied a servant who was going to cut down an old tree. Whilst the servant was making preparations for his hard work, the child seized the large sharply-ground axe; but being too weak to wield it properly, the heavy, upraised axe fell unfortunately across his left hand, so that the whole of the thumb and three-quarters of the forefinger were cut off; the latter remaining hanging on by a little bit of skin. The child was immediately brought back to his mother. When she saw him covered with blood, carrying his thumb in one hand, and holding on the forefinger, the poor mother cried out: 'Holy St. Joseph in the Oak, if you do not heal my child, he will be maimed for life!'

The doctor who was called in declared: 'These two fingers will never heal—it is impossible, and even if they should possibly do so, he will never be able to use them all his life.'

It was only by the persistent entreaties of the mother, who

never wavered in her confidence in St. Joseph, that the doctor was at length prevailed upon to bind up and properly arrange the cut fingers. How great was his astonishment, when after several days he untied the bandages and found that both the fingers were beginning to heal.

Some months afterwards, the principal feast of St. Joseph in the Oak took place. When Father Louis was returning to his house, a lady spoke to him, showing him at the same time the hand of her little boy.

'Father Louis, I have been seeking you for some time to show you what St. Joseph in the Oak has done for my child. I was so afraid that later he would not be able to be a priest, which is a privilege which I always desired for my child and besought of God.'

The priest again examined the little hand; the scar was still deep, broad and red, but the finger was quite pliant and flexible, and nearly well again. He led the little *protégé* of St. Joseph into the midst of the assembled priests and other persons, and all present united in a fervent act of thanksgiving to God and St. Joseph.

Such was the early history of this deacon, and it is only one of the many instances which might be related concerning St. Joseph in the Oak.

33. CURES IN BÖHLE.

In the parish of Böhle, in Westphalia, in the diocese of Paderborn, the devotion and confidence of the parish-priest to St. Joseph have been rewarded by many miraculous cures and graces. We will relate two or three of these.

In the year 1868 on the 4th of October, a blind gentleman

from Utrechct (Holland) was in Böhle, who besides his blindness had a difficulty in breathing. Having returned home, his difficulty of breathing disappeared, and he could read the finest print without spectacles. A year later he returned to Böhle and presented the parish-priest with a richly gilded silver ciborium, undoubtedly the most beautiful in the district, as a lasting thanks-offering for this wonderful cure through the intercession of St. Joseph.

The sister of a parish-priest in Holland was in Böhle on crutches, and had one leg shorter than the other. When she went home she threw away the crutches, as the short leg had been miraculously lengthened.

The proprietor of a refreshment-room in a railway-station had the gout so badly that he could neither walk nor stand, and could not be touched without suffering great pain. He let himself be taken as well as he could to Böhle, invoked St. Joseph with great confidence, and was immediately cured, so that he could return home without pain or trouble.

In the year 1867 a gentleman was in Böhle with his son, who had been blind five years, and had amaurosis in both eyes. After a few days he could suddenly see, and is entirely cured.

34. MIRACLES THROUGH ST. JOSEPH'S CORD.

The Bollandists relate the following wonderful cure, confirmed even by a Protestant doctor.

An Augustinian nun at Antwerp, suffered for more than three years such intense pain that she often fainted through it. Her state was such that the doctor declared that her death would inevitably ensue. She betook herself immediately to St. Joseph, wearing during her invocation a cord dedicated to him, and made a Novena with her sister in his honour. On the 10th of June, 1659, the last day of the Novena, she knelt, nearly fainting with pain, before a picture of St. Joseph; whilst she besought him for her health, her pain suddenly ceased, and she lived seven years after without ever again feeling anything of it. When in the year 1842 this wonder became more public by being read aloud in the church of St. Nicholas at Verona, where the month of March was first dedicated to St. Joseph, many sick persons procured for themselves cords similarly blest, and through them obtained not only health, but also other remarkable graces.

In consequence of this, at Verona, on the 19th of March, 1860, the Confraternity of the Girdle of St. Joseph, which was approved by Pope Pius IX., was, with the consent of the Church, raised to an Archconfraternity, and enriched with many Indulgences.

35. Confidence in St. Joseph's Intercession Rewarded.

On the 9th of June, 1871, Ludwig Lanca, of Miglie, wrote the following to the editor of the *Divoto*, an Italian newspaper:

A peasant's son, eighteen years old, was seized with a dangerous illness. It was a violent typhoid fever, which, in the judgment of the attending physician, left very little or no hope at all of recovery, if there were no change after two days. The third day broke, and the state of the patient had become so imminently dangerous that, by the advice of the doctor, the last Sacraments were administered to him. In their distress the family betook themselves to St. Joseph, whose picture was honoured in the house. Scarcely had they begun to say the Litany, when the patient seemed to awake out of a deep sleep, and desired them to give him the picture of St. Joseph, that he might kiss it, saying that the Saint had promised him the longed-for grace of health; and from that moment he recovered so rapidly, that in three days he was perfectly restored and well.

36. 'ARISE! YOU HAVE SUFFERED ENOUGH.'

We take the following from the periodical entitled 'The Client of St. Joseph':

For nearly five years a strange and painful illness attacked a healthy girl named Mary Borchi, and caused her parents, who had used in vain all the arts of medicine, unspeakable grief. The child suffered from interior paralysis, with frightful unheard-of pains, and continual sickness. Several days passed without the invalid being able to take any nourishment. At last the paralysis seized also the left side of her body, and by the end of August of the following year the unhappy girl had lost her hearing as well as her speech; her hands were drawn together with cramp, her stiffened limbs had lost all feeling—in a word, she lay like a corpse on her bed of pain. But her simple faith had not suffered, and was her one consolation in the midst of such acute agony. While she, deaf and dumb, could hold no conversation with her loved ones, her weary eyes were often raised to a pious picture hanging on the wall of her little bedroom, representing St. Joseph and the Holy Family. She looked upon St. Joseph as her only hope, and though her lips refused their service she prayed to him from her heart, and a voice within her told her that she would be heard. And where else indeed could she have found relief? The doctors had exhausted their experiments, her parents could only shed tears, and expect every moment that death would snatch her from them.

The poor girl was in this state on the night of the 14th of March of the same year, when at about one o' clock, and no one being in her room, she thought she heard a voice which said: 'Rise now, you have suffered enough.' She thought that she was dreaming, or that, possibly, one of the family said it to her to encourage her, and she remained motionless; then she lost consciousness. But when, an hour later, she opened her eyes as one who awakes from a deep sleep, she saw that she was no longer in bed, but on a sofa that was near, supported with cushions, and—O wonderful!—she perceived she had obtained again the use of hearing and speech, and she was easy and flexible in all her limbs, which no longer retained any trace of paralysis, and also had regained all her former abilities; in a word, she was entirely cured. Moved with the most lively gratitude, she threw herself on her knees before the picture, and in prayer awaited the morning, to show herself cured to her mother and the rest of the family. Who can describe the astonishment, the exclamations of joy, the embraces, the tears of such a moment?

All honour and praise to St. Joseph, through whose mediation this illness, which for years had resisted all medical art, was conquered and driven away.

The young girl is now in continual and perfect health, and has already several times, without the least exertion or effort, been to Church and thanked the Most High for such a complete miracle.

We have communicated nothing but the truth, and, indeed,

much less than the truth, in these simple words, in which all must see a new example of how powerful a protector is St. Joseph the Spouse of Mary.

37. St. Joseph Saves a Child.

The 'Semaine Religieuse' of the diocese of Vannes relates the following wonder, how St. Joseph favoured a little boy named William Le Gall.

It was on a Thursday, the 19th of February, at half-past eleven in the morning, and several children were playing in the street, when a heavy waggon, loaded with furniture, drove up. William, all engrossed with his game, did not even perceive the approach of the horses, until one of them actually touched him. He then tried quickly to escape to one side, but being frightened, stumbled against a stone, and fell right in front of the waggon. The driver could not suddenly rein in his horses, which were going at a sharp trot, and the wheel of the waggon passed right over the child's body.

The excitement of the other boys and the passers-by may be imagined; the whole scene took place in a moment, quicker than we could describe it. Many kind persons went at once to raise the child, whom they expected to find quite dead. But before they could do so he was already on his feet. All his companions cried out:

'He is dead! He is dead!'

Now although the little fellow was standing on his legs, perfectly uninjured, all these exclamations scared him, and he cried out in his turn:

'Perhaps I am dead, perhaps I shall die, but I must see mamma again first.'

And with these words he ran home with the greatest speed.

When his mother saw him crying she thought that he had been quarrelling with one of his companions, and prepared herself to give him a wholesome reprimand; but when the boy exclaimed, 'A waggon has run over me!' the poor terrified mother broke into violent weeping, especially as the persons who had followed him confirmed his statement. But little William, whom they immediately began to undress, took a picture of St. Joseph, which he had had in his pocket when the waggon went over him, and said:

'Do not cry, mamma; I shall not die: St. Joseph is with me.'

Then he related that, at the moment when he saw himself in danger of being crushed, he thought of St. Joseph, whom his mother had taught him to love, and pronounced his holy name. He had felt that a heavy weight had passed over him, but nothing more.

The doctor who was summoned, declared that the child had suffered no injury, only a rather dark mark on the skin showed the trace of the wheel.

On the following day, and later on, the boy showed with joyful pride the little picture of St. Joseph to all his acquaintances, and said:

'It was this that saved me.'

When he received a sou from the Sisters of St. Joseph at Cluny, he said:

'I shall not spend this sou, but I shall give it to St. Joseph;' so saying, he went in and laid it at his feet.

His mother conceived a sincere veneration for this great Saint, had recourse to him in all her misfortunes, and although she was poor, offered him little presents, mostly by the hands of her son. Without taking the above related occurrence for a miracle, we content ourselves with communicating it to the honour of St. Joseph.

38. Relief from a Pecuniary Embarrassment.

'Some years ago,' writes a person to us, 'I was in the greatest distress and perplexity; a numerous family, and a series of heavy necessary expenses, brought me into great difficulties.

'My wife, children, and myself all worked unremittingly, but could not get out of our trouble. I endeavoured, by making several loans, to recover my business, but the high interest on which I reckoned was my ruin. Our resources were exhausted, and so was also our courage. After a consultation we determined to sell our business house and to live on the purchase money.

'In order to sell it advantageously we resolved to pray every day to St. Joseph. We persevered in this prayer for six months, and at last, moved by our tears and many petitions, as well as by our misery, St. Joseph heard us, and that in two ways; first he procured me a secure loan of 2,000 francs for a year, and he also sent a good purchaser for the house. Thus were our debts all paid, and our painful situation relieved.' All thanks to St. Joseph!

39. A Lost Paper Found.

A lady writes thus:

'A fortnight ago I lost an important deed of capital to the value of 10,000 francs. In our circumstances this was a most terrible loss.

'What made the thing worse was, that my husband had entrusted this deed to my care, and I had every reason to fear his just displeasure.

'In my distress I had recourse to St. Joseph, and promised to publish it in the monthly periodical called the "Propagateur," if I found the lost paper through his favour. After long and fruitless searches the paper came to light in a most unexpected manner. I thanked St. Joseph with the deepest gratitude, feeling how truly I was indebted to his intercession for this favour.'

40. THE CORD OF ST. JOSEPH.

Angélique Brixard, *née* Francillon, of St. Etienne de Crossey (Voiron Isère), offers her humble thanks to St. Joseph for the favour of a remarkable cure she has obtained through his intercession.

At the end of July of the present year (1884) she was ill, bedridden, and could scarcely move. Her pains were exceedingly severe, and as the physicians could give her no relief, she betook herself to prayer, praying herself, and obtaining the prayers of others.

When she had been about five months confined to her bed, a large abscess formed on her left side, which was lanced by the two doctors who attended her; immediately afterwards a fresh tumour showed itself on the hip-joint, and the doctors declared the bone to be diseased; the pains she suffered were unendurable, and believing her end was approaching, she received the last Sacraments, and took leave of all her friends, endeavouring to console them, especially her husband, who was in despair at the thought of losing her.

Just at this time when her sufferings and illness were at their worst, she received from her brother, who was the Chaplain of the Sisters of Our Ladye of the Holy Cross, a letter containing a *'cord of St. Joseph.'*

'Gird yourself with this cord,' wrote her brother to her; 'tomorrow I will begin a Novena in honour of St. Joseph, the Spouse of the ever Blessed Virgin; the Sisters of Charity, who feel deeply interested in you, will redouble their prayers during these nine days, and I will also solicit others to unite with us.'

Her husband and children likewise began the Novena with great confidence, and they girded her with the precious and holy girdle.

Their confidence did not go unrewarded. Even on the second day of the Novena her sufferings had begun to decrease, an abscess which the doctors had decided to lance disappeared as if by magic, to the great surprise of her physician, who could hardly believe his eyes.

At the end of the Novena, though she still suffered and was weak, yet she was getting really better, and all danger of death was past; since that time her state has daily improved: her left leg, which had become contracted, and shorter than the other, became longer again, and she was able to walk without difficulty. Thus was confidence in St. Joseph rewarded.

41. St. Joseph Rewards Persevering Confidence.

During the month of March, multitudes of devout souls venerate St. Joseph, and are accustomed to ask the Foster-Father of Jesus for some particular grace. And how many of the faithful have seen the confidence they have placed in the most pure Spouse of Mary rewarded in a remarkable manner. We ourselves are acquainted with a pious soul belonging to the better classes, who recommends all her petitions to the great Patron of the Catholic Church. In the year 1884 she became ill and quite unable to perform her duties, which up to that time she had fulfilled with the greatest exactitude. The evil increased to such an extent, that at last she was not able to move without experiencing pain. It was feared that the spinal marrow was affected. In this distress the lady herself, as well as many of her friends, who were most anxious for her recovery, had recourse to St. Joseph. The month of March was approaching, and it was resolved to offer up the devotions to obtain the desired cure. Many approached the Holy Table, and many Novenas were made to procure help for the severely-tried lady, but all in vain: the disease, instead of decreasing, seemed to gain ground. Nevertheless, the sick person did not lose courage or confidence. She used to say: 'It seems to me that it does not yet please St. Joseph to intercede for me, and so God will not answer my prayer.' She continued to pray to St. Joseph saying, 'Hail, Holy Joseph! help me; thou knowest that I only desire my health in order to labour for others, and especially for youth.'

After suffering violent pains for a whole year, she commenced another Novena, begging her friends once more to join her in prayer. When, behold! she began to grow better, and in a few weeks was able to leave her sick bed.

In a short time she was again the providence of her neighbourhood, visiting and comforting the poor and afflicted. If anyone asked her how the happy change had occurred, she would say:

'No one but St. Joseph cured me; I have not invoked him in

vain.'

42. From Olden Times.

Sister Johanna of the Angels, Prioress of the convent of the Ursulines at Laon, in France, was seized with a dangerous pleurisy; she was at death's door and already given up by the doctors, when she was suddenly restored in a most wonderful manner.

This extraordinary case was examined by the Bishop of Poitiers, who confirmed the truth, and published an account of it in the year 1637. We will let the Sister to whom it happened relate the fact in her own words:

'I was, as a dying person, lying in my last agony, bereft of the use of all my senses, and able to control only my reason. In this state I had a vision of a large and bright cloud, in which on one side sat my Guardian Angel, under the appearance of a youth of eighteen years, his head adorned with golden locks, and a lighted candle in his hand.

'On the other side was the glorious St. Joseph, with a face that shone like the sun with superhuman majesty; he appeared as a man between forty and forty-five years of age; the hair of his head was beautiful and long, of a chestnut brown colour. He smiled kindly on all who were around my bed; then turning to me, he bent over me, put his right hand on my side and anointed it with oil, or some other liquid. I felt that my side was wet, and in the same moment I knew that I was well, and said so to those around me.'

Sister Johanna of the Angels then immediately arose from her bed, in which she had lain in a dying state for a fortnight, after having been bled nine times and quite tortured by the pain in her side.

All who saw this instantaneous cure were amazed, especially the doctor, who was not a Catholic, but a Calvinist. When he entered the room and saw the bed empty, and all on their knees, and the Sister coming to meet him smiling, and in her habit, he stood still with astonishment, and ended by saying:
'With God nothing is impossible.'

43. ONE OF ST. JOSEPH'S LATEST FAVOURS.

Not far from Triest stands a poor, very poor orphan asylum. A good Capuchin Father is the founder of it; it is an old solitary house overlooking the bay. The care of this modest home is entrusted to an unpretending honest woman, by name Giovanna. Two or three of her elder pupils remain with her in order to help and assist.

Thirty orphans were maintained and provided for in this house, and besides this they received religious instruction, and were taught reading, writing, and arithmetic, and also the necessary skill in sewing, knitting, washing, ironing, cooking, and gardening, in order to fit them later to take good situations.

I remember the exact date when the following occurrence took place; it was on the 11th of January, of this year (1886). One of the youngest children, Antoinette, had been ill for a long time. It was a wearisome illness. To express myself shortly, I will only say that the pains in her head, stomach and chest were so great that she often beat the suffering parts with both her hands, and tore in pieces the clothes that were near her. The doctor as well as the priest wished to have her taken to the hospital, but the good Giovanna earnestly begged them to desist from this idea. The child was still too young for the reception of the holy Sacraments of Penance and the Holy Eucharist, and it was only with difficulty that the priest could perform the last anointing. I heard that while he was performing this ceremony she tore his stole, which came near her hands, into shreds.

Finally, after a few days, she lay there motionless, her arms crossed on her breast, apparently unable to see, hear, feel, or speak.

Her tongue projected out of her mouth so swollen that it was a wonder how she could still breathe; her teeth were buried in her tongue, so that they were covered by it, and seemed as if they would bite it in two. The two elder girls above mentioned watched two and two alternately by the dying child. The priest and doctor were both of opinion that she could only last a few hours. Nevertheless, this state was protracted from Monday until Friday, and during all this time they were unable to put any nourishment into her mouth.

All at once there was a cry heard in the house; it came from the children who were watching. All hastened to the sick room.

Antoinette had raised her hands from her nearly lifeless body, and made a motion as if to write. They brought her holy water, which she did not touch, but continued to make signs that she wished to write. Then they gave her a pencil and paper, and she wrote, with a trembling hand:

'I see a procession of men, like princely soldiers in red, and their leader is an old man who carries a crown and a lily.'

Repeatedly during the morning she made signs to write, and when they gave her a pencil and paper she wrote always the same words. After a time those in the house again heard the children call, and all again assembled in the room. There sat little Antoinette upright in her bed with closed eyes, and whispering:

'Jesus! Jesus! Joseph! Joseph!'

Then she stretched out her hand as if to take something invisible from an unseen person, and rubbed her eyes with it, first one and then the other. Then she took a part of it, put it into her mouth and ate it; then she joined her hands together, and prayed and opened her eyes. When she saw them standing around her, she began to jump like a child, and cried out:

'I am cured! I am well! Saint Joseph came to me and told me to rub my eyes with the lily, and eat a piece of it, then to pray. Now I will get up and dress myself, and go down to church to thank him at his altar.'

The poor little orphans all fell on their knees around her, exclaiming:

'A miracle! A miracle!'

Giovanna, whom I have known ten years, confessed to me that she was quite overcome with the impression; but that she wished to keep the child back in order to avert a possible disappointment.

'Antoinette,' she said, 'you must not speak, you must lie down; the doctor said that you were to keep perfectly still.'

But the child laughed.

'Oh, that is not necessary now! I am cured and well; I must dress myself and go down; he told me to do so,' and she ran round the room to get her clothes together.

When they saw how well she was, what a fresh colour she had, how bright her eyes were, her tongue rosy-red and small again, and without any trace of being bitten, they brought her something to eat, dressed her, and took her into the chapel, and joined with her in making thanksgiving.

At this time they were expecting the doctor, and the child wished to open the door for him herself, only Giovanna ordered that she was to sit on the bed and wait for him. When he entered the room he asked:

'Where is my little patient? Have you sent her away? Is she dead?'

'Here I am!' she cried, radiant with joy.

The doctor stood for a moment as if petrified, and for five minutes spoke not a word. They related to him all the above-mentioned circumstances, whereupon he made the following declaration:

'I am not a Catholic, yet I feel myself obliged to declare that yesterday I affirmed that, humanly speaking, it was impossible for this child to live another twenty-four hours. Yes, even if I had succeeded in some measure in restoring her health, she would still have remained deaf and dumb and blind, and, at most, imbecile; for she had suffered from a very severe attack of brain fever.'

In the meantime his lordship the Bishop had been sent for, and he came with many others to see her. I myself was a long time alone with Giovanna and the child, and heard the story from both of them. The child is still so young and innocent as to wonder why anyone should want to see her. His lordship the Bishop wishes the month of March to be kept here with great solemnity, and that on the 19th, the Feast of St. Joseph, the child should be allowed to make her first Communion.

I will mention two more circumstances which made a deep impression on me.

Lately I had this little child alone with me, and she came and leaned herself against my knees. Her bright black eyes appeared for a while full of gratitude, then she said:

'Signora, when you wish to obtain anything from St. Joseph, say to him, "St. Joseph, thou friend of the Sacred Heart of Jesus," and he can refuse you nothing.'

The other circumstance I heard from Giovanna.

'Signora, everyone is so astonished at this miracle; but our poor house is a continual living wonder. We are thirty-seven, thirty-three children and four nurses. We have no money, often not a kreuzer (about three-quarters of a penny) in the house, and sometimes know not how we shall get our breakfast the next morning; but then there comes a little present from some client of St. Joseph, with an alms; and so we live in God's hands.'

All who have the honour and love of St. Joseph at heart will welcome in this simple statement a new and powerful inducement to confide, firmly and sincerely, all their troubles to the intercession of this glorious Saint.

III.
St. Joseph our helper in Spiritual Necessities.

1. St. Joseph a Good Missioner.

THE foundation of the mission of Mandera, near Bagamoyo, in the Vicariate Apostolic of Zanguebar, in Africa, is in a particular manner the work of St. Joseph. The Reverend Father Baur, Apostolic Vice-Prefect of Zanguebar, wrote the following account concerning it:

'It was in the year 1880. We desired much to establish a station between Bagamoyo and Mhonda. Therefore I undertook a journey to find a suitable village for a Christian settlement. Father Machor accompanied me. I recommended the journey to the protection of St. Joseph, and we carried with us a relic of the Saint to protect and lead us aright. The 19th of March, the Feast of the Saint, was fixed upon for the day of departure.

'After we had celebrated Holy Mass, we set out for Udon, to which district Mandera belongs, and which is inhabited by poor savages, who are worshippers of fetiches, and also cannibals. A great part of our journey lay though this country, which had never before been visited by any Europeans. We were *not* eaten up! still, we were told from time to time by the natives that we seemed likely to be delicate, tasty morsels, and if we would allow it they would be very pleased to make an experiment of the flavour of their guides!

'Many of these speeches were made, we believe, as grim

jests; all the same, they were not very comforting to us. However, we bore them with as good a grace as we were able, but each time any question arose concerning a settlement in the country we were met by a decided refusal. I saw that nothing could be effected by human means, and so I said to St. Joseph:

' "Thou art our Leader; for the glory of thy Divine Son, thou has laid open to us this country, and the merciful designs of God have shown us the needs of these poor souls. Now, therefore, do whatever thou wishest, but with regard to us, we will return only when the site of the future mission is decided upon."

'And so we continued our journey without knowing whither we were travelling: going on at random, straying about from one village to another, always hoping, yet never succeeding, from one chief ordered to another; until, at last, in Holy Week, we arrived in the territory of a chief named Kingaru. The village was called Mandera.

'As soon as Kingaru caught sight of us, he stopped, took a step backwards, uttered violently some guttural sounds, shook his head, looked at us again, and the more he gazed the more numerous became the manifestations of his surprise, until at last he burst out into the following speech:

' "Hear my words, hear! This night, whether I was asleep or awake I know not, but I saw before me a beautiful old white-haired man, who touched me as if he would awake me, and then he said to me:

' "Kingaru, look! There are two white men and a little caravan coming to thee; receive them kindly, and give to them all they desire.'

' "And it was you two, you two—thou and thou, whom I see before me. Ha! how does this happen? How is this possible?'

'And without leaving us time to utter even one word, he called all the people of his village, and exclaimed to them, "Look here! these are the two white men whom I saw last night with the beautiful old man, as I told you this morning when I arose. Look! Here they are!"

'The good people looked at us with great surprise. We ourselves, at first also astonished at the behaviour of the chief, soon found the key to this mystery. St. Joseph had interposed in our behalf, and from the depths of our hearts we thanked him while we asked him to continue his kind mediation until the end.

'After the first emotions of excitement had subsided, I announced to Kingaru the purpose of our journey, and asked him for some portion of land in his dominions.

' "All that I have belongs to you," answered the worthy man. "My house is yours, my fields are yours, my people are yours; take what pleases you, only remain with me."

'We stayed there, indeed, for eight days, and kept the Feast of Easter in this unknown village, shown to us and entrusted to our care by St. Joseph. During the whole time Kingaru endeavoured to bestow on us every mark of kindness and attention. He gave us shelter in one of his huts, provided us with sheep, fowls, rice, bananas, and everything we could desire in the way of food, showed us different parts of his territory, pointing out the best situations, and loaded us with proofs of his respect and attachment.

'As soon as the site of our house was fixed upon we departed, but Kingaru insisted on being himself our guide, and would not leave us until he had brought us again safely to the frontiers of Udon. Truly this good and simple African belonged to the number of those whom Almighty God, according to the opinion of St. Thomas of Aquin, would sooner send an Angel to give them baptism than allow them to perish.

'A fortnight later he visited me in Bagamoyo, and as the time drew near to begin the building he came once more—this time accompanied by a numerous retinue to accompany the missioners and to carry their baggage.

'His devotedness towards us is still unimpaired; he is now a fervent Christian, and each day, with man of his people, assists devoutly at the Holy Sacrifice.

'Thus has St. Joseph acted for Mandera. To him be praise, honour, and thanks!'

2. STRANGE!

In the year 1843 a professor of the Society of Jesus, in Sitten (Wallis), became ill. The young religious, distinguished by talent as well as by virtue, felt death approaching. The Rector of the College was Father Theodore Neltuer, well known throughout Switzerland, France and Germany by his Apostolic labours.

When it became his duty to administer the last Sacraments to the dying Father, he was the more moved, as he had only lately lost two other members of his community.

After all the touching rites were concluded he went up to the bedside, and in a tone of paternal authority ordered the Father, as soon as he entered heaven, to claim the intercession of his great patron, St. Joseph, in order that a worthy substitute might be sent to fill his place in the Society. The dying religious promised, and soon after his soul passed away on the 6th of July.

Now what came to pass?

In the autumn of the same year twelve novices presented themselves, and eight of them bore the name of 'Joseph.' Three more 'Josephs' shortly followed.

And among the number of these was reckoned the famous Father Kleutgen.*

3. A Touching Conversion.

The following account was sent from a reliable source to the 'Propagateur,' concerning a touching conversion at Cannes, in the south of France, which was the work of our glorious Saint:

'In the beginning of the year 186—I gave to a pious lady two copies of "The Devotion for the Seven Sundays of St. Joseph," who immediately commenced making them.

'A poor woman, the wife of a workman came one day to see her, and told of the grief she was in on account of her husband, who had for many years neglected his religion, and all her efforts to convert him had hitherto been fruitless. Then this good lady advised her to have recourse to St. Joseph, and to keep the seven Sundays in his honour, giving her for this purpose one of the above-mentioned copies.

'The poor woman thanked her and began this salutary devotion with great fervour and confidence, which increased more and more the nearer she came to the end of it. At last, in the seventh week, firmly relying on the support of the holy husband of Mary, she made a firm resolution that she would

---

* This name, so renowned in Germany a few years ago, may not be so well known to our English readers; but we did not like to change the text of the original.

dare a last attack, and speak once more on a subject which she had been long forbidden to even name.

'To encourage herself, she armed herself, if I may say so, with a picture of St. Joseph, and one day, holding it up before her husband, she said to him gently:

' "O mon cher ami, if you would only take refuge in this blessed Saint, I am convinced that he would obtain for you the grace of returning to God."

'To her intense surprise and great joy he took the picture from her hand, looked at it thoughtfully, then kissed it reverently, and finally said that he would go to confession at once.

'He carried out his good intention faithfully, and received the Sacrament of Penance with good dispositions and many tears, which were a proof of his sincere contrition and desire of amendment. The holy season of Lent was drawing to an end, and a retreat for men was being given in the town. This true convert, followed all the exercises with great fervour, and at the close of it had the happiness of once again receiving Holy Communion.

'Full of courage, he made a few days later a public pilgrimage of thanksgiving to the "Chapel of Redemption," a short distance from Cannes; and from this moment he never again relapsed into his former irreligious life, often suffering in preference great inconvenience, and making many sacrifices in order to be able to assist at Holy Mass on Sundays and holidays. And he always attributed his return to God as a grace from St. Joseph, and esteemed the simple little picture which his wife had been inspired to show him, more than anything else he possessed in the world.'

4. A Lost Son Found Again.

Our only son at eighteen years of age failed to pass his examinations. In consequence such a deep melancholy and depression gained possession of him, that he persuaded himself that his failures must have been owing to some weakening of his mental faculties, and that he should never be able to finish his studies. He wished to choose another state in life. We believed this to be only an imagination, and so refused our consent.

A few days afterwards he secretly left us, without saying one word of what he intended to do. When he did not return home that evening, we felt a sad presentiment that our child was gone for ever.

The police were at once acquainted with the circumstances of the case, and every possible means was used to discover the fugitive, but in vain. No trace of the lost one was to be found. His unsettled state of mind led us to fear that he might have been tempted to make away with himself, and for ten whole months we lived in indescribable grief and anguish.

'What can have become of our poor boy?' was the question his mother and I asked ourselves from morning to night.

The 16th of May, 1881, was the day of his flight; on the 13th of March, 1882, two Little Sisters of the Poor came to our house to solicit alms. On this day I had been more than ever depressed, and I felt a kind of yearning for the sympathy and assistance of another, so I confided my affliction to these good Sisters, entreating the help of their prayers.

'We are in the month of St. Joseph,' said one of them; 'if you would address yourself to him with confidence he would certainly aid you. Our community shall begin a Novena this evening; unite with us, and I am sure that on the feast of St. Joseph you will receive news of your son.'

I joined in this devotion with more earnestness than I had ever before prayed, though I did not venture to consider myself worthy of so prompt an answer to my prayer; yet only a week after the visit of the two nuns we received a letter from this beloved son whom we were beginning to mourn as dead. It was dated from England; in it he asked our pardon for having left us, and begged to be allowed to return. And on the 23rd of March we had the happiness of once more embracing him. His letter had been written on the eve of the Feast of St. Joseph.

He immediately resumed his studies, and after a time successfully passed his examination. Still better, never again has he caused us the least anxiety; and we, his parents, never pass a day without thanking St. Joseph and recommending anew to him the care of our child.

5. St. Joseph helps in every Distress.

A Benedictine nun writes the following:

'St. Joseph is always kind, always merciful, but sometimes he appears to be even lavish and prodigal in the manner of bestowing his graces. In gratitude to this great patron of the interior life, I must relate the following account:

'A young girl belonging to a good and highly-esteemed family had received a careful education, yet did not seem to have reaped the desired fruits from it, for as she grew to the age of womanhood she gave proofs of great levity of character, and many other serious defects.

'The mother, who loved her child tenderly, grieved exceedingly; and in her perplexity as to the wisest course to be pursued, sought the advice of one of her relations, a pious and sensible lady, who recommended her to place her daughter under the special care of St. Joseph, as the best advocate in all matter concerning our eternal salvation. The mother followed her counsel, but it need hardly be said that the young girl herself had no idea of the many prayers on her behalf which from that day were unceasingly presented before the throne of God, by the pure hands of His earthly Foster-Father; yet she soon felt a great interior change coming over her. Her thoughts became more serious; she began to be tired of worldly amusements, to despise vanity in her dress, and the frivolous conversation which had hitherto proved so attractive to her now became distasteful.

'Gradually, but very gradually, she improved in every respect; virtue now delighted her as much as it had formerly repelled her, she followed the better inspirations of her soul, and soon her happy mother could say: "I do not know how it is, but my child is so wonderfully changed."

The fidelity to these first graces was a sure means of procuring others. This soul, so dear to St. Joseph, was enlightened more and more, until it received from God the privilege of a call to the religious life.

'This, which had formerly been her greatest antipathy, became her only desire. Generously despising all difficulties and treading under foot all the worldly delights to which she had once devoted herself, she entered a religious Community, and is to this day an example of every virtue.

'Thanks to St. Joseph! her happiness is his work.'

6. A GOOD INSPIRATION.

'A short time ago,' so wrote a student to the Reverend Father Huguet, 'I was on the eve of a most important examination in jurisprudence; it was a Government examination, and as I am naturally timid, I was very fearful about the result, notwithstanding the great exertions I had previously made.

'Feeling very much disquieted, I at length made a resolution to recommend myself in a special manner to St. Joseph, promising him to make my gratitude public if he granted me the wished-for success.

'Reverend Father, the results exceeded my expectations. I never lost my presence of mind at the examination, and in spite of the questions being often both puzzling and complex, I passed through all in a satisfactory manner. To show you how plainly this proceeded from the protection of St. Joseph, I will relate a fact to you which I am ready, if necessary, to confirm by oath.

'On the eve of the examination I suddenly seemed to see distinctly, one after another, all the questions that would be proposed to me the next day. I said without hesitation to a relation who was with me at the time. "To-morrow I shall be examined on such and such subjects." Nevertheless, I was afraid of relying too much on a presentiment of this nature, knowing that young people are liable to illusions on such occasions. At the same time, as I thought St. Joseph might possibly have a hand in the matter, I resolved not to let it pass unnoticed.

'The important day arrived. As I said before, I felt no fear, and was able to answer all the questions fluently. Wonderful to relate, these questions were exactly the same as those which had come into my mind so distinctly the day before. By this I recognised the whole extent of the protection of St. Joseph. In communicating this fact to you, I fulfill my promise; and if others in my situation should experience the same difficulty, I advise them to apply to St. Joseph, when they will certainly obtain a happy result.

'B. BALLAND, 1884.'

7. THE LITTLE FIRST COMMUNICANT.

A parish priest, in whose district infidelity causes great corruption, relates the following touching experience:

It happened last year when the children of the parish were in retreat preparatory to their first Communion. They were peacefully assembled in the church around the pulpit, like young lambs around their shepherd, while I, as the pastor, was administering to them the spiritual food of the word of God in anticipation of feeding them with the Bread of Angels.

The little assembly was listening with silent attention, when suddenly a man dressed like a workman entered. With sparkling eyes and an angry countenance, he ran first to the right side, then to the left, casting searching and scrutinizing glances everywhere.

I quietly and gently asked him:

'What do you want, my good man?'

With a rough voice he answered:

'I want my child.' The words so harshly and loudly uttered evidently caused great disturbance and fear among my little flock. Each one looked anxious and troubled.

'Sir,' continued the man, 'I demand my child, and at once.

His mother is a Catholic, but I am not, and my son shall never be one either.'

'You surprise me, my friend,' I replied. 'We never receive a child to instruction for its first Communion if its Catholic Baptism is not most clearly registered. Was not your son baptized in the Catholic Church?'

'Yes.'

'Were his god-father and his god-mother Catholics?'

'They were.'

'Had you not given your consent?'

'At that time, yes; I was present.'

'Well, my friend, is not your son still a Catholic?'

'Until now, I acknowledge he has belonged to the religion of his mother, but from this moment he must belong to mine.' With these words he seized the boy, whom I had previously brought up to him, and shaking him by the arm, in a furious tone exclaimed: 'Go along! out with you; from this day forward you will have to deal with me!'

The poor little fellow cast on me an imploring look, and with tears he whispered:

'O please, do not forsake me!'

I then tried to place myself between the child and the enraged father. All present were terrified, and feared that I might become a victim of his violent passion. In their excitement and anguish, many sobbed and cried aloud. But no harm happened to me; the man even appeared somewhat to quiet down.

Now we become witnesses of a most touching incident. The dear child fell down on his knees, embracing his father's feet, and in a voice broken with emotion and tears, but full of childlike tenderness, he said:

'Oh, my father! I will always be obedient, I will love you with all my heart; but, I beseech you, allow me to remain in the religion of my mother!'

His words became choked and inaudible, and I feared he would faint.

It was a heartrending scene! All were in tears, the other children wept unrestrainedly. Yet the father's heart, hardened and faithless, was insensible to the dictates of natural affection.

But he was sufficiently subdued to agree to wait until the conclusion of the instruction and devotions before forcing the child to go along with him.

After the sermon, I saw the boy pale and trembling.

'You are afraid, my dear child?' I said, and I took his hand.

'Oh, certainly,' he answered; 'I am afraid, but mostly for my mother. She will surely be ill-treated this evening.'

'Go quietly with him,' I said; 'be very good and obedient, and trust in God.'

He went. Not without painful compassion did I see him walk away by the side of his father like an innocent lamb, which follows where it is led, dumb and without resistance.

When he was gone, we all knelt down together, and said a prayer for him, hoping much in favour of this matter, which had so direct a claim on the mercy of God.

Yet our hope seemed to be in vain.

The next day the retreat was continued, but one place remained empty!—the boy did not come.

What had happened? An eye-witness afterwards told us.

When the father and son returned home, the man raised his arm to strike his wife, but the child left him no time: he sprang up, clasped his arms round his father's neck, embracing him with all the power of love; and with many tears besought him in the most ardent and tender manner to spare his mother, and to allow him to make his first Communion.

The arm of the father dropped again from very shame; yet his hatred for religion remained undiminished. The next day he took the boy with him to work, and kept a watchful eye over all his movements. A deep sadness now seemed to settle on the poor child; he wept day and night, and could not eat. He heard the bell daily summoning his more fortunate companions to their religious instruction, while he alone was debarred from sharing in their joyful preparation. Each stroke of the bell increased his sadness; as the Psalmist says: 'His heart and flesh were pining away for the Altar of his God.'

The Feast of St. Joseph was the day chosen for the first Communion.

I glanced over the lines of children, all dear to my heart, and noticed with pain the absence of the one little figure, even more loved by me than all the rest, because he was so sorely tried. His place was still vacant.

'Oh, my Jesus!' I sighed, 'Thou surely wilt not let this chosen lamb of Thy flock perish!'

All at once there was a stir among the ranks—something seemed to have happened. The bright faces of the expectant children grew more joyful still, and I heard whispers: 'There he is! there he is!' And, oh! thanks to God and St. Joseph, my eyes rested again on the beloved child, whom I had been so deeply mourning. His face was pale, bearing traces of his past sufferings, but his countenance was peaceful and serene, and as he approached the Holy Table to receive his Lord, he looked sweet and pure as an angel.

How had it happened?

The boy, when taken away by his father, had, like us, had

recourse to St. Joseph, and the glorious Saint had taken this innocent child's heart under the protection of his Lily Sceptre. He had hidden this young confessor under the folds of the mantle which he had encircled Jesus in his flight into Egypt.

The irreligious father had been overcome by the Holy Foster-Father of Jesus, and had yielded to his son's desire; and thus we had the joy of seeing him return to us free and happy.

8. THE STORY OF A CONVERSION.

Listen now, how a young spiritualist has been converted by means of a medal of the pure Spouse of the Blessed Virgin Mary. This fact was communicated to me by the young man himself.

Emmanuel T——was born near Cognac (Dep. Charente), and had the misfortune of losing his parents, when he was scarcely twenty-one years of age.

Finding himself the possessor of a considerable property, he set no bounds to his luxury and extravagance. In Baden alone he lost in a short time more than 100,000 francs at the gambling tables. Also being a fervent apostle of spiritualism, he left no means untried to win disciples. I had often occasion to see him, and the sight of this poor youth running headlong in the path of destruction, moved me to exceeding pity for him.

One day when he was just setting off on a journey, I gave him a medal of St. Joseph, saying to him at the same time, 'Take great care of this medal; it will entitle you to the protection of which you stand so much in need.'

Six weeks later, this medal was destined by the mercy of God to be the means of saving this erring soul from everlasting death.

At Montelimar, Emmanuel was attacked by a strange and severe illness, suffering much from violent spasms and attacks of suffocation, such as he had never experienced before. While he was lying one night on his sick-bed, the eyes of his soul were suddenly enlightened: he seemed to see the abyss of hell open before him, and threatening to engulf him, and he thought he heard the roaring and scornful laughter of the devils.

He called for the servant, who was sleeping in the next room, but he could not make himself heard. As he believed that his last hour was come, he wished to burn certain private letters, and with much pain and difficulty dragged himself across the room to fetch them out of the pocket of his cloak. While looking for them, he happened to come across his medal of St. Joseph.

It was a sudden inspiration! He pressed it to his heart and lips; he conjured the glorious Patriarch to ask pardon for him of Almighty God; he promised to convert himself, and to go to confession that very day, if the life which he had so misused and misspent should be spared.

Oh miracle of Divine mercy! Oh wonderful power of St. Joseph! how prompt you are in coming to our aid.

Scarcely had this unfortunate man, who had been struggling for six hours with death, called upon St. Joseph, then he fell into a gentle and refreshing sleep. In the morning when he awoke he found his medal still pressed to his heart. As he had promised, he made a very sincere confession—the first for ten years.

Afterwards, actuated by a spirit of thanksgiving and desire of doing penance, he undertook a journey to the Holy Land. This pious pilgrimage was followed by others to Loretto, and to La Sainte Baume, in order to venerate there the tomb of the model and patroness of penitents.

Finally this converted libertine and atheist made his home near Lyons, where we believe he still lives, leading a holy and exemplary life, beloved alike by God and man.

9. THE SUCCESSFUL EXAMINATION.

A pious lady living in Paris, filled with zeal for the honour of St. Joseph, and having had personal experience of the great graces bestowed by this Holy Patriarch, wrote thus to Père Huguet:

'I am full of confidence in St. Joseph, and have I not reason to be so? Are we not daily witnesses of the most encouraging and wonderful occurrences?

'Some days ago the wife of an officer came to me to complain of her great trials, and, indeed, I have often had occasion to compassionate her on account of the bad treatment which she receives from her worthless husband.

'The lady herself is a good Catholic, and just now the point of dispute was regarding their son, a youth about seventeen years of age, who, in consequence of a chest disease, was rather behindhand in his studies. The father, only anxious that he should pass certain examinations for which he did not as yet feel ready, tormented the poor boy unceasingly, without any regard for his weak health.

'As the best comfort I could think of, I gave the lady two medals of St. Joseph to sew into the clothes of her husband and son, and began a Novena in union with several other persons, the last day of which was to be on the 18th of September, the very day of the so much dreaded examination.

'The morning arrived only too soon, and as his father still insisted on his at least making the attempt, the boy appeared, pale and trembling, among the ranks of the other competitors. Naturally, he was far from being equal to them, but he had with him a heavenly protector, whom perhaps none of the rest thoughtless, eager young crowd had thought of invoking for light and aid. His mother, when she bade him farewell, consoled him and encouraged him, saying confidently: "Go, my child, in obedience to your father, and God will bless you! You will pass your examination well, as many devout souls are praying for you to Mary and Joseph."

'The mother's words were a true prophecy, and in the evening he returned home happy and successful, and full of gratitude as well as astonishment; for, as he confessed, he could not possibly have answered questions on subjects which were almost unknown to him unless he had a very special grace and assistance.

10. St. Joseph Saves Two Clerics from the Conscription.

Two young clerics, who were in the Ecclesiastical Seminary at Toscana, became liable to be called upon for military service. Both were poor, and their parents were unable to provide the sum of money necessary to procure substitutes for them. In their distress they felt inspired to commit the matter to the care of St. Joseph. They therefore united in prayer with a certain number of their friends, and made a vow, the conditions of which they promised to carry out if they were freed from the obligations which threatened them. Humanly speaking, there was not the very least hope of their escaping the conscription; on the contrary, they had every reason to expect to have shortly to change the 'soutane' for a soldier's uniform!

Time went on, the dreaded day drew nearer and nearer, and St. Joseph gave no sign to lead them to expect deliverance. But he was only withholding his help, to test and to strengthen their confidence. For so it was that it happened in a very remarkable but perfectly regular and lawful manner that before the day for drawing for the conscription came the names of both these young men were struck off the lists.

Upon hearing this, they not only fulfilled their vow with great joy, but took every opportunity of publishing this favour of St. Joseph, in order to encourage others to place confidence in the intercession of this great Patriarch.

11. A High Number.

'On the 21st of January, 1882, the conscription took place in our town,' so writes a schoolmistress, 'and it became a day of sorrow for many a mother's heart.

'At the commencement of school that morning a little girl of seven years of age threw herself into my arms bathed in tears.

' "Oh, Fräulein!" she cried, "my mother is weeping so much; she fears that my brother will be taken for a soldier, and I am so sorry."

' "I share in thy sorrow, my child, but we must say, 'the Will of God be done' in all things."

'After a few moments of silence, the child suddenly lifted up her little head: a smile was on her lips, a ray of hope shone through her tears.

' "Let us ask St. Joseph to take care that my brother should draw a good number. Oh! how I will love St. Joseph, if he will do this, and how I will tell everyone about his kindness."

'She spoke so fervently, her little hands clasped tight together, as if she fully expected to get all she desired now that she appealed to St. Joseph.

'When the usual time for prayers came, I told the children about the trouble of their little companion. Never was prayer made more fervently. Just as we were concluding, the great clock of the church tower struck ten.

' "That is the hour, Fräulein," exclaimed all the children in a breath. Both looks and hearts of all turned towards the statue of our good Father. "St. Joseph, thou friend of the Sacred Heart, pray for us." So prayed the little ones. And at that very time the brother of the little girl drew one of the very highest numbers, and so escaped military service.

'Who would not recognise in this more than a mere accident? Who will not acknowledge in it the powerful influence of St. Joseph?

12. THE LAST DAYS OF ONE CONDEMNED TO DEATH.

At the Assizes in A——, the year 185—, a man guilty of highway robbery and murder was condemned to death.

The circumstances of his crime were of such a frightful nature that the jury could find no reason to moderate the sentence, nor to recommend him to mercy. At first the prisoner obstinately denied his guilt, but as proof after proof was brought forward, he became silent.

He heard his sentence with a stolid, hard indifference. When the judge exhorted him in moving terms, to try and prepare while he had time, for his judgment at a higher tribunal, it seemed to make no impression at all upon the unfortunate man. Silently, and with an expression of obstinate stubbornness, he suffered himself to be lead out of the hall of justice to the cell of the condemned criminals, into which he was locked.

The crime the unhappy man had committed seemed to have the effect of brutalizing him completely. No persuasion of the priest who was chaplain of the prison, could induce him to speak; every effort to soften him seemed as ineffectual as if he had been made of stone.

Some pious nuns, who, to the great satisfaction of the Government, took care of the criminals, did all in their power to break through his obduracy; but all was in vain. Dumb, morose, and sullen, the poor wretch sat in one corner of his cell, and could be induced to pay no attention whatever to anything.

'Prayer is our only resource,' said Sister Veronica to the other nuns; 'in this case no human power can avail. It is terrible!'

And the good Sisters did pray more for this poor man even than for any of the other criminals, his case seemed so desperate.

One morning, Sister Veronica when she came to the cell, set down the water bottle which she had brought, took a small hammer from out of her girdle, and a nail from her pocket, and proceeded, without saying a word, to fasten a little picture of St. Joseph to the wall. She noticed that the prisoner was for the first time watching what she did attentively, so as she turned to go away, she said:

'That is a picture of St. Joseph, the patron Saint of the dying.'

Whatever hopes the transient arousing of his attention may

have awakened, seemed doomed to disappointment. The prisoner relapsed again into his dogged indifference—nothing roused him, nothing touched him. When the Sister brought him his dinner, the picture hung on the wall untouched, and the prisoner sat crouching in his corner. The kindly words the Sister spoke were unnoticed, excepting that once she heard him give a deep sigh, as with his head resting on both his hands he sat staring at the ground. This went on for many weeks, for it happened that the ratification of the sentence of death was unusually long in coming. The Chaplain often came and conjured with the unhappy man to seek reconciliation with God, but he could not get one word in answer to all his exhortations.

The Sisters prayed more and more fervently, but apparently without success.

At last the confirmatory judgment arrived, and the second day after its reception was that fixed upon for the execution of the criminal. All the particulars were arranged; the officer in charge proceeded to the cell of the condemned man to inform him that the ratification of the sentence had come, and to try to awaken him to the fact of the terrible earnestness of the hour so fast approaching for him. Sister Veronica told the officer before he entered the cell that he would find a great change in the prisoner—that for the last few days he had seemed quite another man, although he had not yet broken the silence he had preserved ever since his condemnation. When the official and his attendants entered the cell they found the unfortunate man sitting in his usual attitude, but the dull, obdurate expression of his face had given place to a look of quiet mildness. He appeared to take no notice whatever of those who came in, nor gave the slightest sign that he even understood what was going on.

Not even an eyelash moved when the officer read out the day and the hour fixed for his execution. At length looking up, he said:

'I knew that it would be one day this week, and I thought it would be Friday.'

The official then began to persuade him to prepare himself to die as a Christian.

'Have I not already told you that I knew that I must die this week; since I have known that, you may be sure I have been preparing myself. I need no exhortation from you, Herr Procurator. You have done your duty, that is sufficient.'

The officer was startled.

'What do you say, you knew?' he asked with surprise.

'That I had to die this week,' was the answer.

'Since when have you known this?' he questioned further.

'Since Monday I have known it,' replied the criminal.

The officer put his hand to his head in perplexity. He had the document containing the royal confirmation of the sentence in his hand; it had only arrived late the previous evening. He had not said a single word to anyone about it till that morning. How could the criminal in his solitary cell have had certain information concerning his execution since Monday? Casually he glanced down the parchment; it was certainly strange and very remarkable. The royal signature was dated. Last Monday! How could the prisoner have received an intimation of his fate?

'It is not possible that you can have known this since Monday,' exclaimed the officer excitedly; 'his Majesty only signed the warrant on Monday. How, then, could it possibly have been known to you?

'I have known it,' replied the prisoner quietly; 'how, is another matter,' and here for the first time he changed colour, his eyes moistened, and sought the ground.

He had risen, and had been standing while he spoke; now he fixed his eyes upon the little picture of St. Joseph, and seemed to go through some sharp conflict within himself. After some moments, turning to the officer, he said:

'Yes, I will tell you how I came to know. It is wonderful enough for a man like me, you will say, but still it happened. And I thank God it did.' He sat down again then, as if he could thus relate better what he had to tell. 'I have deserved death—the sentence pronounced upon me is just. But to know that I had to die soon whilst in full health, and not to know when, *that* was what I could not bear. That it might be to-morrow, or might not be for weeks; that any day it might be announced to me that I must die to-morrow—but not to know for certain. This uncertainty was what was so terrible to me. All that the priest said to me from the beginning was true, but it only tormented me, because of the agony of the uncertainty. I did not know when, but only that I had to die—it was this that made it so bitterly hard. Then one day the Sister fastened that picture to the wall. St. Joseph, the Sister told me, was the patron of the dying, but she did not know that he was also my patron Saint. Ah! I have thought a great deal since I have been in here—a great deal of both good and bad. But up till that day it had been chiefly bad. But then came remembrances of how, when I was a child, I had been taught to reverence my patron Saint! Ah, if I had only done it, I should not be here now! When the Sister left me I went up to the picture, stood before it, and looked at it as at something that in my childhood had been dear and holy to me. After a time I gathered confidence and began to pray very quietly. But the terror that was upon me, of the uncertainty of the time that the death that was so certain would come upon me, was more than I could bear. Suddenly! That it should come quite suddenly was my fear. If I only could know *when* it would be—if only I might know for certain just a few days before—then I thought I would try to prepare in earnest. But I did not know when it would be, and when I did know I should not have time to prepare. So it came into my mind to ask of Almighty God a special grace through the intercession of St. Joseph. The priest had said that the mercy of God was beyond measure infinite, and that if the sinner only approached Him in the way He had appointed, nothing could limit His mercy. So I asked St. Joseph to obtain for me a sign when I was to die within a week.'

'And what was the sign?' here broke in the officer.

'Oh, it was a very simple sign,' continued the prisoner. 'Up to that day the same Sister who had fastened the picture to the wall had always brought me my dinner; if one day another came in her place, then, so I thought, I should consider it a sign from St. Joseph that in that week the affirmation of my sentence would arrive. And so it happened. Last Monday a strange Sister brought me my dinner. By that I knew how it stood with me, and at once began to prepare myself for death. So you see that God deigns to hear even the greatest sinners if they turn to Him humbly and with contrition, especially if they have the help of so powerful an intercessor as I had,' and he pointed gratefully to the picture of his patron Saint, 'whose aid I certainly have not invoked in vain!'

All this was uttered by the criminal with such a calm assurance, such a perfect resignation, that it seemed as if he took it all as a matter of course. He now begged that the priest might be sent for, and that he might be left alone with him, 'to close his heavy account definitely,' as he expressed it.

The officials thereupon departed, not a little astonished and touched at the change that had taken place in the once so hardened criminal. Before they left the house, Sister Veronica was, however, sent for, to be questioned as to whether the change of Sisters, so significant to the prisoner had really occurred or not. The good Sister was no less surprised, when the officer repeated the story related to him by the prisoner, than he himself had been upon first hearing it.

'Last Monday!' and Sister Veronica thought over it for a moment—'Last Monday; oh yes! he is right, I remember it all now; it was last Monday that just as I had reached the door of his cell with his dinner, and was only waiting for the gaoler to open the door, Sister Clare came running to fetch me, saying that the Superior wanted me directly. So I put the dish of food into her hands to take in to him whilst I went off to our Reverend Mother. Thus it happened that for that once I did not serve the prisoner myself. There was no other reason. And so after all it really was St. Joseph!' she exclaimed. 'It was like an inspiration my thinking of putting up that picture on the wall, and now I can understand the alteration in his manner since Monday. May God be for ever blessed.'

She then fetched the Reverend Mother that she might hear these particulars from the officer. The Chaplain was called for at once, and he was told how it was with the prisoner, and what had happened. He listened with great surprise, but shook his head, as if he could not credit so great a change in one who had for so long remained obdurate. But nevertheless he hastened to the cell of the condemned, and found him on his knees before the picture of St. Joseph. He then related again in short to the priest what had happened, and maintained a firm conviction that he might indeed yet hope for grace since God had so graciously deigned to give him the sign he had asked for.

Then it also came out that the poor man had been far from unmindful of his soul from the first moment of his condemnation, and that not one word the priest had said during his repeated exhortations had been lost, but treasured up and laid to heart. But nothing until the granting him that sign, as he called it, had unlocked his heart.

And now, already prepared, he made at once a general and contrite confession. During the rest of that day he hardly let the priest out of his sight for a moment. Early the next morning he assisted at the Holy Sacrifice of the Mass in a most edifying manner, and with an abundance of tears received Holy Communion. He then prayed with the priest and all present, that he might have courage and strength to go through the last painful journey he was so soon to take.

He was then led out into the court of the prison, where the guillotine awaited him. His step was firm, and his look tranquil; and he expressed such deep contrition and resignation that all present were more edified by the Christian fortitude he evinced than terrified by the awfulness of the spectacle.

13. A Miraculous Oil Lamp of St. Joseph.

We have received the following account from Riemange near Trieste:

'A church here, which is attached to the parish of Dolina, was originally dedicated to St. George, but in it was an altar dedicated to St. Joseph. In earlier times there existed also a large confraternity in honour of the glorious Foster-Father of Our Lord Jesus Christ. This had been established and confirmed by Pope Innocent XII., in 1693.

'That this confraternity was very large and devout, is proved by numerous answers to prayer, attested by ex-votos which still remain. As also the existence of a miraculous oil lamp which used to burn before the altar of St. Joseph, and is still at the present day to be seen hanging before the high altar of the church, which has been newly-erected in honour of St. Joseph.

'Concerning this miraculous lamp there exists an old document, written by the parish priest of the time, which relates the following occurrence:

' "For some time," so it runs, "a rumour had been prevalent among the people that the lamp hanging before St. Joseph's altar was always found to be alight and burning brightly, in spite of its having been again and again extinguished. The parish priest appeared to take no heed of the report at first, but nevertheless, he thought much over this strange occurrence, and determined to have the matter thoroughly investigated and proved. He therefore sent for the parish priest of Dolina, and called the churchwardens and some others together. They all went to the church, the sacristan put out the lamp carefully, every approach to it was securely shut and fastened up, the church doors locked and sealed, and all was carefully examined, in order to secure that no entrance to the church was possible. The parish priest of Dolina took charge of the keys, and gave orders to the churchwardens to watch the church with all possible care, and if through the grated and barred windows they should perceive a light in the church, immediately to inform him. After some time of careful watching the lamp was observed to be again burning; this was on the 27th of March, 1749. At once the parish priest was sent for, the doors, seals, and barricades were all examined and found untouched. The Bishop was informed of the fact, and before him the witnesses deposed on oath to the truth of these statements."

'In consequence of this miraculous event, the church was rebuilt and dedicated to St. Joseph, and the confraternity then took a greater extension, as may be seen from the register of names of members. The last name was registered in 1828, since then the confraternity seems to have died out; but devotion to St. Joseph still exists among the people, and especially on the eve and day of his feast, when the church is crowded with devout worshippers and pilgrims.

'It is much to be desired that this confraternity should again revive, and that devotion to our dear Saint, the star of the nineteenth century, should spread and take deep root in the hearts of the people.'

14. THE FEAST OF ST. JOSEPH—19TH OF MARCH.

As each year comes round, St. Joseph grants us fresh graces on his feast. We could wish that our little work could this year carry our thanksgiving abroad throughout all lands for his favours have been greater and more numerous than ever.

St. Teresa, the saintly foundress of so many convents of Carmelites, has in her writings borne the following testimony to efficacy of the intercession of St. Joseph, and her testimony is indisputable. She writes thus in her life:

'For the celebration of the Feast of St. Joseph I exerted myself with the utmost fervour. My greatest desire was that it should be kept with all possible grandeur and solemnity. For by this time I knew something by long experience, of the greatness of the honour in which he is held by God. Would that I could persuade the whole world to honour him by an especial cultus! I have always observed that people who have a true and practical devotion to St. Joseph succeed in the acquisition of virtues much more rapidly than others, for this heavenly protector takes a very great interest in the advancement of those souls who recommend themselves to him. I have myself, for many years past, always asked him for some particular grace on his feast-day, and I have never asked in vain.'

One of the most pious of the daughters of St. Teresa, who tried as closely as she could to follow in the footsteps of her beloved Mother, was the Venerable Mother Anne of Jesus, who, when sent to France, burned with a like desire to glorify St. Joseph. After the opening of the church of their monastery at Dijon, in the year 1637, upon the first occurrence of his feast she determined to keep it with all the splendour possible.

The Blessed Sacrament was exposed for the day, they had beautiful music, a celebrated preacher was invited, an immense congregation assembled; in fact, she did everything she could think of to make the Saint's festival glorious.

After the solemnity was over Our Lord let His Spouse know how pleasing this feast had been to Him, and that He wished that it should be celebrated each year with equal pomp, and also that her action had obtained many graces for the house, both special and general. Her Divine Master likewise assured her that souls of extraordinary sanctity, and possessed of great spiritual gifts, should be called to that house; and the after-history of the convent bore ample testimony to the fact that the prediction was fulfilled.

Thus Mother Anne of Jesus inspired all with great devotion to their glorious protector. Every day he was invoked by the Community for special graces. One grace in particular they always asked for, namely that no postulant might be received into the Community who would prove afterwards unfaithful to her vocation, and this favour has always been accorded to them in a very marked and astonishing manner. For Divine Providence has so ordered that several times, candidates who at first were considered most eligible, and would have been regarded as decided acquisitions; either on account of their connection, or spiritual gifts, or great fortunes, have either been unexpectedly refused, or else have themselves changed their minds at the last moment. And each one of these cases proved subsequently, that St. Joseph had been active in his protection of the monastery.

The 19th of March brings to us also the remembrance of the death of St. Joseph; at least it does so if we allow ourselves to be influenced by the very old and pious tradition which ascribes the event to this day.

Let us therefore, go back in spirit to that long past time, and let us silently enter the little house of Nazareth, at the very moment when the soul of St. Joseph took his departure from this world.

Our Divine Redeemer Himself closed the eyes of this 'Just one,' and after having accomplished this duty of love, He wept sweet tears of tenderness and affection over His Foster-Father. The Immaculate Virgin mingled her tears with those of her Divine Son. Oh! what a favoured death-bed; watered with the tears of a God-Man, and with those of the Mother of God!

The venerable body of the deceased lies there, as if already in part glorified. Surely never before had such a look of sublime repose rested upon any countenance. His limbs were still as flexible as in life, and an odour sweeter than that which has ever since been diffused from the bodies of any of the Saints, perfumes the air. For never was sanctity comparable to the sanctity of St. Joseph.

Whilst silence and devotion reign beside this holy corpse; whilst Angels bend to look upon it with rapt admiration; whilst Jesus and Mary give expression to their gentle grief, let us draw nearer to the mortal remains of the holy Patriarch. And first let us with reverence venerate this noble head which was found worthy to be initiated into the secrets of God, and to which the confidences of the Omnipotent were imparted; this head, which had to endure such anxious thoughts, such harassing cares, anxieties, and afflictions in connection with the secret Incarnation of the Word of God; this head in which the thought of God, and of His glory, ever reigned pre-eminent, and into which no shadow of a thought contrary to the law of God ever gained admittance; this head, which during the Sacred Infancy so often supported that of the Incarnate Word, which thus resting upon it, cast as it were some of its own glory over it, crowning it in some sort with a diadem from His Divinity; this head, which, as the last sigh escaped his lips, was blessed and honoured by the kiss of the Son of God!

We salute thee! Oh! blessed head which in Heaven is now crowned with so glorious a crown!

Let us now approach the feet of the Holy Patriarch. Let us kneel and reverently kiss those holy feet; every step they took was either for the love of God, for Jesus, for the ever Blessed Virgin, or for us.

And lastly, let us venerate those glorious hands which lie folded so meekly upon his breast. Their day's work is done;

never will they have to labour more except it be in distributing those favours and graces which Jesus and Mary through them, bestow on us from Heaven.

With faith and love, let us press our lips upon those holy hands, and oh! let us, in anticipation of that last hour so soon approaching for each of us, entreat the protection of those strong arms of St. Joseph. Nay, let us do more; let us fly for refuge to his heart; let us hide ourselves within its inmost recesses, and beg him to protect us, both during life, and in the hour of our death.

Let us say to him as Jacob said to the Angel of old: 'Non dimittam donec benedixeris mihi.' 'I will not let thee go until thou bless me.'

And as this grace of a good death, and entrance into Heaven, is one of such vital importance to us, let us after we have fervently besought St. Joseph's protection, turn also to Jesus and Mary. Let us not lose this moment, we are sure to gain a hearing now, see, while they still weep over him, whose eyes they have just closed. Let us plead with them. 'For the sake of him you mourn, for the sake of St. Joseph, for the sake of his sweet death, for the sake of the tears you have mutually shed, we beseech and implore you, O Jesus and Mary! in union with St. Joseph, bestow upon us your blessing for our last hour. O Divine Redeemer, O merciful Virgin Mother! keep for us, we entreat you, one such glance of pity and loving compassion, as you have just bestowed upon the dying Joseph, with which to bless us in our last agony.'

IV.
St. Joseph our helper in the hour of Death.

1. St. Joseph the Patron of a Happy Death.

OUR readers, doubtless in laying before St. Joseph their various necessities have pleaded often for that, the most important of all; the grace of a happy death. Indeed as St. Joseph died in the arms of Jesus and Mary, he is very naturally honoured and invoked as the special patron of the hour of death. Innumerable histories aid in confirming our confidence in the intercession of this glorious Saint, as the patron of a holy death. We will here first relate a beautiful instance which was told to us as fact by a friend, in the year 1879.

'Joseph Carvalho, a Brazilian, was my fellow student at the Jesuit college at Feldkirch; he was descended from the family of the Marquis of Pombal who acquired such a sad celebrity by his unjust persecution of the Portuguese Jesuits. This youth having returned to his country, fell into a consumption and after having been for some time confined to his bed in the house of his guardian, felt the unmistakable symptoms of death approaching. Joseph then begged most earnestly that he might have the assistance of a priest; but his guardian, who was a determined and inveterate Freemason, would by no means allow any priest to be admitted into his house.

The dying youth upon hearing this, was much grieved and distressed, and finding himself deprived of all human hope he had recourse in his extremity to prayer, and most fervently invoked his dear Patron St. Joseph.

Soon after this is a merchant presented himself at the house of the heartless guardian, and requested to speak with the invalid; as no suspicions were entertained he was admitted into the sick room; after a short conversation he discovered himself to Joseph as a priest and a religious.

'I have heard,' he said, 'of your distress, and that you so longed for the help of a priest. I am come to receive your confession.'

The poor young man made his confession, and the priest having given him absolution, promised to return in two days, and bring him the Holy Viaticum.

When he came, however, on the second day, he found only the corpse of the poor lad.

But surely St. Joseph who had so mercifully procured him the benefit of the one Sacrament to protect him in his dying hour, will have continued to assist him, and will, we may hope and trust, have helped him to make a holy and peaceful end.

2. THE LAST MOMENTS OF A PAPAL ZOUAVE.

The following is the account of the death of Joseph La Saige de Villebrun, Lieutenant of the Papal Zouaves, which was sent by his brother, who was a volunteer in the same regiment, to his family:

'MY DEAREST MOTHER,

'Whilst still under the impression of this terrible event, I cannot help communicating to you some particulars relating to the last moments of Joseph's life. They are, indeed, of a nature to console the heart of any Christian mother.

'At the foot of his bed Joseph had placed a statue of St.

Joseph, together with a little statue of the Madonna. One morning he was observed to gaze fixedly upon these objects for a long time, absorbed and motionless, excepting that his lips moved from time to time in prayer. His orderly at last inquired what occupied him so intently. He answered:

' "Go quickly and tell the Sister to send for the Chaplain; let her call him at once. I want to go to confession, and St. Joseph says I must make no delay, as I have not a moment to lose."

'Immediately the Rev. Father Daniel was brought to his bedside, and after hearing his confession (which he afterwards told me was a most fervent one), the priest said to the Sister:

' "I am going to offer the Holy Sacrifice for him, and will after that bring him the Holy Viaticum."

'At first my brother seemed quite contented with this arrangement, but just as the priest was ascending the altar, Joseph again sent him an entreaty to come, saying it would not do to wait till the end of the Mass, as by that time he would have lost his consciousness, which he would never recover.

'The priest most kindly came at once, and Joseph received Extreme Unction, joining in all the prayers, and after he had received the Holy Communion, he made acts of love and fervent thanksgiving to God for having granted him the grace of being conscious in this the last action of his life. All those who were present wept, and were deeply moved to see so great a faith in the midst of his acute sufferings. Shortly after this he became delirious; but even in the wanderings of his mind, he still made aspirations to St. Joseph. Being left alone once, only for a few seconds, he was found to have got out of bed and thrown himself upon his knees on the stone floor at the feet of the statue, fervently invoking the Saint. The next day he sank into a state of prostration, from which nothing could rouse him, but the mention of St. Joseph's name.

'The last time I saw him open his eyes, it was to cast one last lingering look upon the image of his dear Patron Saint. After this he seemed to be so much quieter that it was thought he might rally for a time; but no, a few moments only passed and then he breathed a heavy sigh, and all was over, without any struggle or agony, without anyone even perceiving that death had come.

'Yesterday I was introduced to our Holy Father the Pope. One of the papal court acquainted His Holiness with our bereavement, and he addressed some comforting words, and held out his hand for me to kiss.

'He made some inquiries concerning Joseph, and meanwhile some of my friends brought forward a photograph of the dead Zouave, which one of the attendants showed to His Holiness. Pius IX. wrote upon it the words, "*Pax Tibi,*" then raising his eyes to heaven, he said, "*Ita in Paradiso!*" (He is in Paradise).

'The loss of our poor Joseph has been lamented, not only by the whole of the regiment, but also by several Roman families with whom he was intimate.

'I have been earnestly requested to distribute his photographs, and thinking that it would be in accordance with your wishes, I have done so. Joseph has inspired such an universal interest, that this recognition of their sympathy could hardly be refused.'

3. 'I SHALL DIE IN THE OCTAVE OF ST. JOSEPH'S FEAST!'

Since the particulars I am about to relate to you refer to the honour of St. Joseph, you would more naturally expect to receive them from the pen of our dear Sister Aloysius of Gonzaga, than from mine; but, alas, death has entered here.

On the 21st of March she gave up her beautiful soul to God, after she had given us the example of the most elevating spectacle that can be seen on earth—a holy, spotless life, crowned with the martyrdom of terrible suffering. This, our Sister bore with angelic patience, and her death was like to that of those Saints who have rested sweetly in the Lord.

Being one of those appointed to guide her in the paths of sanctification and of perfection, in which she most generously trod, I may say that few have known her better than myself, and I may truly add that in her were found the most brilliant intellectual talents, together with a childlike faith, and a perfect innocence and simplicity.

She has passed through the world without being tainted by its evils, as of old the three children were preserved from the flames of the fiery furnace at Babylon.

Her religious life counted only thirteen years and six months, and yet her course in religion may be called a long one, for all her days were well filled, both by fighting against herself, and by her self-sacrificing devotion to the welfare of her neighbour.

This treasure which death was so soon to take from us, was known to us more fully during her last illness, which lasted several months, and during which she had to endure the greatest sufferings. Delicate scrupulousness, humility, patience, a detachment from all earthly things, and a longing for heaven; such were the revelations of these last months of unspeakable suffering.

She had always entertained a great devotion for St. Joseph,

and eagerly sought to gain others to love him. Indeed the Arch-confraternity of Angers has largely reaped the fruits of her zeal in promoting the honour of the great and Holy Patriarch.

'I shall die in the octave of his feast,' she said to me some days before the 19th of March. And as I have said before, she gently departed on the 21st of the same month, after receiving from her superiors the permission to die. 'For thus to die in obedience will be much more beautiful,' she said to the Reverend Mother.

The little altar which she had erected to St. Joseph, and adorned in her cell during the month of March, was left until the corpse of our beloved Sister was removed; and in the choir the temporary altar of St. Joseph for March had to be changed in order to make room for the coffin.

These circumstances are all touching when we remember what a tender devotion she had towards St. Joseph.

4. 'BEHOLD ST. JOSEPH IS COMING TO FETCH ME.'

'You will most likely remember that among our school-children we had a little girl who was a protestant, the niece of General N— —. By the assistance of the Blessed Virgin and St. Joseph it was arranged for her to remain with us, although after the death of the General, her relations made every effort to take her from the Convent.

During the fifteen months of her stay here, the child had acquired a deep devotion to St. Joseph. She was always displeased whenever it happened that in the chapel the image of this her dear Saint was less adorned than that of the Blessed Virgin, and she also frequently spoke of St. Joseph with great love.

Her most ardent desire was to receive Baptism and to make her first confession; but as she was born of protestant parents, and as besides all her family were protestants, it was thought necessary to wait until she had attained her fourteenth year before allowing her to do so.

Shortly after the Epiphany she fell into so dangerous an illness, that soon every hope of her recovery was given up. Now the poor child could not rest until she had received the Holy Sacraments of Baptism (conditionally) and of Penance, and had been anointed. Shortly after, indeed the very day following her fourteenth birthday, she received Holy Communion with great fervour in presence of some of her relations.

All the time of her illness the sick child had suffered patiently, but from this moment she became a real model of gentle resignation.

From the first she had rejoiced at the prospect of going soon to Heaven, and one of her most joyful anticipations was that she should see and know St. Joseph. Her unshaken devotion to him was rewarded in a wonderful manner.

For two days we had been expecting her death, when on the Wednesday she suddenly raised herself upright in her bed and with a beaming countenance exclaimed:

'Look, here is St. Joseph coming to take me away!'

I inquired: 'Where is he?'

She pointed with her finger, but words failed her to describe the Saint's appearance distinctly. She only said: 'he was most beautiful, that she saw him resplendent and surrounded with radiant light.' She conversed aloud with him for about a quarter of an hour.

Once she requested me to move a little to one side that she might see him better, and she said he beckoned her to follow him. It was extraordinarily touching to hear with what simplicity she conversed with him, earnestly begging him not to go without taking her with him. She preserved her consciousness to the last moment, and then quietly lay back on her pillow and breathed her last. It was a sweet death! St. Joseph will certainly have presented this innocent and pure soul to his Divine Son.

The confessor of the convent and the parish priest, to whom I related this occurrence, both declared that undoubtedly this little child had seen St. Joseph before her death. As for me, I can never forget her countenance, beaming as it was with joy; even death could not mar its beauty. And I feel certain that henceforth the whole house will make a point of keeping the feast of St. Joseph with greater honour and devotion than ever, and that all will seek his intercession with redoubled confidence.

5. An Edifying Death.

On the 23rd of March last year, a young girl died, who had spent three years in the boarding-school of Notre Dame de Charité. During the first two years C. X. had shown a rather disagreeable character, but lately the wholesome effects of a retreat had manifested themselves in her; she gave herself more to prayer; and the habit of pious recollection, and other improvements indicated a change in her disposition.

Her mother came to visit her on the 25th of February and finding her a little indisposed proposed to her to return to her home. Without much consideration, she at once agreed to the proposal, and immediately informed her companions that she was going to leave school. On the 1st of March, however she became worse, and was obliged to keep her bed. It was then that the words of one of her mistresses recurred to her mind:

'My child, will not the world be injurious to you?' She pondered over this thought and considered besides all the good advice that she had received, especially concerning prayer; these reflections weighed upon her heart, and at last she made this generous petition to St. Joseph.

'Oh! my dearest Father, if you forsee that I shall be lost in the world, let me rather die at once.'

On the 6th of March, the doctor declared that her recovery was hopeless, as rapid consumption had set in. The sick girl, who had guessed as much, asked her mistress to tell her without disguise what the doctor's opinion had been. The good nun hesitated:

'Mother,' said the child, 'I am going to die; I have prayed to God through the intercession of St. Joseph, that it might be so, and I feel that my prayer has been heard.'

Her eyes were dimmed with tears, and on being asked whether she regretted the loss of her life, she replied:

'Oh no! for I well know now, that I could not have saved my soul in the world.' From this moment she could not help expressing to all, the happiness she felt at this sudden change in her destiny. At the last, however, a great trial caused her some moments of disturbance. The inmost wish of her heart was to die in the house which had been the means of such precious graces to her soul. On the other hand, her parents urged her returning home at once to them.

'I have good reasons for wishing to die here,' she said; 'they will all pray for me and offer many Communions for me by which I may hope to be freed from Purgatory, and so go sooner to my dear Lord!'

Thrice did the parents yield to their daughter's wish, but the fourth time that they urged their desire, C. X. thought herself bound to submit to her mistress's advice, and to comply with the loving requests of her parents. Perhaps God wanted to console her relations by the sight of the holy and edifying death of their child. So she was taken to her home. Upon the 17th of March, feeling more oppressed, the dying child asked to be anointed, and on the next day she received the Holy Viaticum. Two of her school companions came to visit her on the 20th, and knowing that she so longed to have died on the feast of St. Joseph, they said to her:

'Well, you see, St. Joseph has not taken you as you desired, on his feast.'

'Oh!' she replied, 'it was because he did not think me well prepared enough, but he will certainly take me before the conclusion of his octave.'

Her disconsolate father besought her to ask Almighty God to restore her to health; but she answered:

'I cannot do so, for I have prayed that I might die in order to save my soul, and the good God has granted my petition; I thank Him for it.'

She faced death with a wonderful peace of mind. When the cold sweat burst forth upon her forehead she said to her mother:

'This is the sweat of death, it will not last long now; please bring me my veil, as I wish to be buried in it.'

They asked if she desired that her crucifix which she so frequently carried about her, should be buried with her also.

'No, keep that,' she said; 'the sight of it will comfort you; I have a scapular and my medals, that is enough. Tell the Reverend Mother and my companions, that I shall not forget their commissions!' And being asked by her mother what these were, she said:

'Oh! it is for Heaven. God and the Saints, know well what has been recommended to me!'

In these sentiments C. X. yielded up her pious soul to her Creator. It was on the fourth day of the octave of St. Joseph.

May all pious souls commit all their necessities, and especially the hour of their departure out of this world, into the hands of the great and powerful Foster-Father of our Lord.

6. St. Joseph does not forget His Clients at the Hour of Death.

The following is a touching account of the last moments of a Christian Brother, who during the time he was teaching at Tunis, showed himself a zealous promoter of the devotion to St. Joseph.

Obliged to return to France to recover his health, which had been undermined by the African climate, this true servant of the Holy Patriarch, being ripe for Heaven, entered into his eternal rest. The Superior of the house where this good Brother died, has communicated the following touching particulars.

'Our dear Brother Protegenius came to this house in the beginning of November, 1868. When he beheld our pleasant abode, the solitude of Fonserune, outside Beziers, he rejoiced, saying he hoped here soon to recover his health. In fact he felt a great improvement in it during the first weeks; but, nevertheless, towards Christmastide, the spitting of blood again came on, and he understood that all the skill of doctors was now powerless, so that there remained nothing for him to do but to prepare for a good and holy death.

'He spoke to all those who came near him with wonderful calmness, and evinced a great certainty of the nearness of his approaching end, so much so that he predicted that his departure out of this life would occur on the feast of his dear patron and protector St. Joseph.

'When at last he became bedridden, he requested to have by him a picture representing the death of St. Joseph, and having obtained his wish, he took it into his hands and kissing it most tenderly, exclaimed: "Oh dear St. Joseph! Oh good St. Joseph! remember your promise and grant me the grace to depart on your feast day, and like you to die in the arms of Jesus and Mary!"

'The picture being hung up by the side of his bed, the sick Brother kept his eyes constantly fixed upon it. In spite of our best endeavours to procure for him palatable food and refreshing drinks, he had completely lost all appetite, and his frame became so emaciated that it more resembled a skeleton than a living being.

'It appeared from what he told someone in confidence a few days before his death, that whilst in Tunis, he had in the month of March, 1868, made an offering of his life in order to obtain salvation of the soul of one of his former scholars, who had been seized with brain fever, and was dying without the Sacraments.

'Hardly had Brother Protegenius made this offering to our Lord, than the youth recovered his consciousness, contrary to every expectation of the doctors, and begged to see a Capuchin Father, and having confessed, he received all the last

Sacraments with a contrite heart, and died a most edifying death.

'Meanwhile a very slight indisposition of Brother Protegenius began now to assume a serious character, and at length it prevented him from fulfilling his duties as teacher. It was found necessary to send him back to France, in the hope that his native air would help his recovery.

'But God had accepted his generous sacrifice, and St. Joseph, by whose hands it was offered, gave him the assurance that he would recover no more, but that at the end of the March following he would reach the term of his earthly pilgrimage. When the doctors who attended him tried to lead him to expect his recovery, he thanked them kindly, but no sooner had they left him than he said to the Brothers:

' "We shall see whether the doctors or I have spoken rightly."

'About the middle of February, when the confessor of the Noviciate was about to absent himself for a few days, he proposed to give him the last anointing before leaving; but Brother Protegenius answered with great confidence:

' "Father you may go without fear, because at your return you will find me in the same state as you left me; my hour is not yet come." He gave the same answer when the like proposal was made to him on the 25th of February, and repeated again: "My hour is not yet come."

'On the 28th of February, he received Holy Communion, which favour was granted to him every Sunday. Towards evening he asked that the Brother Superior might be fetched, and said:

' "To-morrow the month of St. Joseph begins, that month in which my dear patron Saint will open the gates of Paradise to me, and introduce me into my heavenly country. I had asked him to let me die on his feast; but in consideration of the disturbance it would cause in the house on that day, it being besides the feast of the Patron of the Institute, and of the Noviciate, my death would interfere with all the arrangements, so I have begged him to let me die on the 3rd of March, which is the first Wednesday of the month, and my prayer has been accepted. If it will suit the Chaplain, I will prepare to receive Extreme Unction to-morrow."

'He received this holy Sacrament with full consciousness, and such beautiful sentiments of faith and resignation, that all present were moved to tears. Towards evening he fell into a state of weakness so great, that we feared he would not live through the night. All therefore remained praying around his bed; he still continued to answer and join in the devotions, and the confessor gave him the indulgence in *articulo mortis*. When these several ceremonies were ended, the dying Brother expressed his gratitude to his community, looking lovingly on each of them, he raised his eyes to Heaven as if to say: "The good God and St. Joseph will reward you for all you have done for me; I am going to them to await your coming."

'Tuesday passed on quietly; he repeatedly kissed his crucifix and the picture of St. Joseph, saying: "To-morrow I shall leave this place of banishment, this valley of tears."

'About twelve at night he sent the infirmarian to rest, and only one Brother remained with him. Towards four o'clock he asked him to hand him his crucifix, and a little statue of St. Joseph, and having impressed on them most loving kisses, he fell into a kind of slumber. The Brother who was watching took this opportunity to go and call the community, on returning, scarcely three minutes after, he found the dear

Brother breathing his last sigh, whilst pressing to his heart the images of his Redeemer and of his beloved patron Saint. It happened just as he had predicted—he died on the morning of the first Wednesday in March. Brother Protegenius was in his forty-fifth year. All his brethren admired the goodness of God towards him, and the wonderful favour which St. Joseph had obtained for him. From that time the novices never mention him but as the beloved servant and client of St. Joseph.

7. St. Joseph obtains for a Sick Person the Grace of Dying in the Arms of Jesus and Mary.

Our dear Sister Joanna, who for six years had been confined to her bed by a grievous sickness, was ever heartily longing for the moment to come when she should go to rest in our Lord. Although she was very suffering, the end did not as yet seem to be near.

About a month ago, writes the Superioress, the doctor appeared even to notice some improvement, and from day to day her nurses shared in this opinion. One day after Mass one of the nuns came to her and said:

'Sister Joanna, do you know what day this is? Is it not Wednesday, St. Joseph's Day?'

'Oh, my dear Sister,' answered the sick nun; 'yes, it is the day of St. Joseph! This day my end must come. Oh, let us pray,' she added earnestly, 'that this may be so!'

The other hesitated a moment, but then replied:

'Several Saints have prayed to God that He might let them die on such or such a day, and they were heard. We may also make a similar request to St. Joseph.'

'Oh yes! And do you ask it,' was the reply.

Then the nun prayed aloud:

'Oh, holy Joseph! grant to my Sister Joanna the grace to die like you, in the arms of Jesus and Mary. Open to her on this day, which is consecrated to your honour, the Gate of Heaven and of the Sacred Heart of Jesus, if such be the Will of God.'

The sick nun repeated every word with ardent fervour, and at the end she said:

'Add—let it not happen in the night.'

The Sister then added:

'Moreover, let it be before night, good St. Joseph, and only grant this prayer if her debts are already paid, and if her crown be already prepared.'

Sister Joanna gave a nod of assent, saying: 'Otherwise I prefer to suffer more here.'

She continued making more ejaculations, and as she was concluding her prayers, the nun who had watched by her in the night came to her and inquired how she felt. Sister Joanna replied that she should probably die that day. The Sister repudiated this idea altogether, and said that on the contrary, she thought she was getting better. Meanwhile, the morning went on, and as the hours passed the hope of the sufferer appeared to change into a strong conviction. When our Reverend Mother, who only left the sick room for business, or her more important avocations, returned to her seat by the bedside, Sister Joanna said to her very confidently:

'Reverend Mother, I shall yet die in this month.'

'How so, this month? Why, do you know what day of the month it is?'

'She replied: 'Yes, it is the 31st, and St. Joseph has whispered to me that I shall die to-day.'

However, no one believed that she spoke seriously, for there was no sign of any change for the worse to be noticed. Still she continued to affirm that she should die that day, and that St. Joseph, with the Blessed Virgin and St. John would come and carry her away. She said to the Reverend Mother, speaking as if from conviction:

'About six o'clock I shall be dead.'

It was then just four o'clock. When the Superioress returned a short time afterwards followed by the priest she found Sister Joanna much weaker; the priest, however, hesitated about giving her the last Absolution, as, he said, nothing looked like the near approach of death, and he should be very much surprised if it were indeed to happen that day. It was now five o'clock. The dear sufferer was silent, and seemed to be wrapt in great recollection; they noticed how intently she kept her eyes fixed on the statue of St. Joseph. Then they asked if she would receive the Reverend Mother's blessing, to which she answered:

'Yes; that I may die in obedience.'

The Reverend Mother stood up at once, saying:

'My dear Sister, if our Lord calls you to Himself, go in peace under the protection of Mary. Nos cum prole pia benedicat Virgo Maria.'

Thereupon Sister Joanna said with a loud and strong voice:

'I am already judged. I shall not have to endure any pains in Purgatory. God the Father has said to me, "Thou art My beloved daughter!" I have seen the Blessed Virgin, St. Joseph, and St. John the Evangelist. This evening the Blessed Virgin and my Guardian Angel will place a crown of glory on my brow. I have delivered a soul from Purgatory. Perhaps I may yet deliver another one.'

Here her elder sister (whose religious name was Mary of the Assumption) interrupted her to inquire, 'Is our dear father in Heaven?'

'Yes, he is in Heaven, but I have not been there as yet. I have not yet presented your petitions to Almighty God, but I shall do so presently. There remains nothing for me but to die. I shall soon die—*this* is easy for me now. Reverend Mother, I have promised to conceal nothing from you, therefore I have told you all. This evening you can tell the other Sisters in recreation; I know that they will all rejoice with me.' Then, upon being asked whether she would like the Chaplain to be called, she said: 'If he would see me die, it is time he should come.'

The whole community now assembled in the sick room; it was ten minutes past five. When the priest came, the Litany of the Blessed Virgin was being recited, and the Chaplain then said the acts of Faith, Hope, and Charity, which the dying nun repeated with him, and several times invoked the holy Names of Jesus, Mary, and Joseph.

'My dear Sister,' said the Chaplain, 'you are already in the Heart of Jesus; in the arms of Jesus; you are resting on His breast.'

'For ever!' she replied.

'Let us now,' he continued, 'say the prayers for the dying.'

'Yes, willingly,' she answered.

While these devotions were going on she appeared to be rapidly growing weaker and weaker, and when the prayers were ended she repeated once more the holy Names of Jesus, Mary and Joseph; then sweetly slept in our Lord without the least struggle or agony. It was ten minutes to six o'clock. The Chaplain, who was present, admired the extraordinary and wonderful grace which our Lord had granted to this His humble handmaid; he intoned the Te Deum at once, before even proposing to commence the usual prayers for the repose of her soul.

This our beloved Sister had shown herself all her life a model of simplicity, innocence and obedience.

This account was written by Sister N— —, of St. Ursula, Superioress of the convent in which Sister Joanna died.

8. A Favour Granted by the Devout Use of St. Joseph's Cord.*

From the Lower Rhine.

A man who had for many years neglected his religious duties fell dangerously ill. His wife entreated him to receive the last Sacraments, but all in vain, and she dared not mention the subject again. Being a devout client of St. Joseph, her piety made her ingenious, and she came to me to have a cord of St. Joseph blessed, and placed it secretly on her sick husband. For the doctors having ordered him poultices, she fastened them on by tying them with the blessed cord round his body.

From the first the poor man felt somewhat better, and though the pains again increased he was more patient and more resigned, and at last of his own accord asked for a priest. He received the last Sacraments with great devotion, shedding tears of joy and contrition. He asked pardon of his wife and children for having through his indifference in religious matters, given them so much disedification and pain, and he

---

* See Appendix, Note.

admonished his children to hold to those religious principles which he, now at the hour of death, embraced, and not to be led away by those opinions which had misled him during his life. He spoke in like manner to all his friends and relations who visited him. But he could not understand how it was that all of a sudden he had become so changed. Whereupon his good wife discovered to him the pious artifice she had practised, and told him that he was indebted to St. Joseph for this grace.

The happy convert shed tears of joy and gratitude, and insisted on at once being inscribed in the confraternity of St. Joseph. Holding the blessed cord in his hands, he repeatedly kissed it, making many loving ejaculations.

Finally he died in the arms of St. Joseph, while his trembling hand was still grasping the picture of the Saint. His last words were:

'Holy Joseph, lead me to Jesus your Foster-Son, and my Redeemer!'

9. A MYSTERIOUS EXPEDITION.

During the night of January 2nd, 1882, a strange old man presented himself at the house of the parish priest of B——, and begged of him to come at once to a deathbed. He explained to him that he would find the dying person, in such and such a house. This old man was quite unknown to the priest, and the street he mentioned bore a bad reputation.

He hesitated therefore—could it be some treacherous snare that had been laid for him? but the stranger again urgently renewed his request.

'It is important that you come without delay, for it is a poor old woman in her agony who wants to receive the last Sacraments.'

A sacred duty had to be performed, so the priest hesitated no longer; he dressed himself with all speed, and followed the unknown messenger. The night was bitterly cold, the old man seemed however not to mind it. He walked on quickly, saying to the priest by way of encouragement:

'I shall wait for you at the door.'

The door at which they stepped led into one of the worst houses of this part of the town, and the priest holding the most Blessed Sacrament in his hand, was at first seized with fear. On second thoughts, however, remembering that Our Lord came to seek and to save sinners, he took courage in the thought that he was but following in the footsteps of his Divine Master, and seizing the handle he rang loudly at the house door. No answer came; he knocked several times but all remained quiet.

The old man was standing somewhat aloof; at last the priest turning to him said:

'You see it is useless, they will not open the door.'

'Let me try,' replied the mysterious stranger, and he came forward while the priest retired a few steps behind him. 'As soon as the door opens,' he said, turning to him, 'step inside as quickly as you can; go upstairs and open the door of the room at the end of the passage, there you will find the dying woman.'

These words were spoken in such an authoritative tone, that the priest could venture no objection. Then the old man knocked in a peculiar manner at the door and immediately it flew open, and the priest entered without difficulty; he walked upstairs, and opening the appointed door, found himself beside the bed of a sick woman, who being in the greatest anguish of soul was continually crying between sobs and sighs:

'A priest! a priest! They will let me die without a priest!'

The servant of God drew near.

'My daughter,' he said, 'here is the priest.'

She could not, however, believe it.

'No,' she said, 'no one in this house would have fetched a priest!'

'My child, an old man called me to your assistance.'

'I know no old man,' she said, looking astonished.

At last the priest succeeded in convincing her that he was indeed the minister of the Divine Mercy whom she desired; and he prepared her to make her confession and receive the last Sacraments of the Church. She accused herself of all that lay so heavily on her conscience—the sins of a long life of transgressions—and expressed so deep a sorrow and contrition, that the priest marvelled to find such a lively faith in a soul which had been so long and so utterly separated from God. He inquired whether she had retained the custom of reciting any particular prayers.

'Only a daily Hail Mary to St. Joseph to obtain a happy death,' she replied.

The priest now prepared everything for the administration of the last Sacraments; whilst he was thus engaged several persons came in and went out of the room without, apparently, seeming to notice his presence. He gave the poor woman the Holy Viaticum, and then anointed her, and did not leave this penitent sinner until she had peacefully rendered up her purified soul into the hands of her Lord.

When the priest left the house to return home he went out as quietly as he had entered, without meeting anyone on the way.

As he was pondering over the circumstances of that night,

and on the blessed mission he had accomplished, he became convinced that the kind and venerable old man could have been no other than the glorious and merciful St. Joseph, the protector of the dying.

10. A Happy Death.

The story which I am about to relate was written to the 'Propagation' of Canada, and took place in New York. I myself read it in an English newspaper, and I think it will edify the reader as much as it has edified me.

About five-and-twenty years ago, near the large and splendid town of New York, in a lonely and desolate spot, stood a poor deserted cottage, which had been built by an unfortunate man, who could find no shelter in that rich and populous city.

The sight of this hut reminded one of the poor stable of Bethlehem, in which our Saviour deigned to be born, being exposed, like it, to every wind and inclemency of the weather.

In this miserable habitation, an unfortunate sailor dwelt alone. He had fallen into the greatest poverty and distress from long continued sickness, and had found no one who would lend him a helping hand.

In the extremity of his misery he was even refused admittance into the hospitals, since he had no one to recommend him, and no one to pay the expense of his maintenance. This poor man, forsaken by all, was indeed greatly to be pitied. What made him even yet more an object of compassion, was the fact that during his long voyages at sea he had entirely given up the practice of his religious duties, although he had not quite lost the faith; but for many, many years—indeed ever since his childhood, he had not so much as once entered a church.

Of all the good teaching of his pious mother, one thing only seemed to remain impressed upon his memory, namely that St. Joseph was the patron of the dying, and that on their departing this life, he would open the gates of Paradise to those who should have asked it from him with confidence. In consequence of this belief, and full of trust in the power of the great Patriarch, he had never let one day pass without reciting three Paters and three Aves in honour of St. Joseph, to obtain the grace of a happy death. On land as well as at sea, in storms and in calms, always and everywhere, the old sailor had been faithful to this one devotion; and now in his poor and lonely hut, when forsaken by all, he was left alone to face death, this practice became his only consolation and comfort. But, alas! as yet St. Joseph had never come to his assistance any more than had any of his fellow-men; he did not appear to take any notice of him.

'Oh! but he will come at last,' thought the poor forsaken man, and he went on praying.

He was not mistaken. One day someone knocked at the door.

'Come in,' said the dying sailor, with a weak and feeble voice; 'Open—enter, oh, holy St. Joseph! for who else would come to me, a poor, miserable and forlorn creature but you!'

And, truly, what happens! not indeed St. Joseph in person, but he whom St. Joseph had sent to bring consolation to the dying man entered. Who then was this? Oh, marvel of love and mercy! It was our Divine Saviour Himself, Jesus in the most Blessed Sacrament, and the priest, His minister, bringing comfort and refreshment to the poor sinner in his last hour.

As may well be imagined, the sailor received the last Sacraments with the liveliest feelings of faith, gratitude, and love; betokened by the tears which, rolling from his sunken eyes, fell down his weather-beaten and withered cheeks.

'Who then told you, Father, of my sad condition? inquired the old sailor of the priest.

'My good friend, it was an old man of venerable appearance, whom I have never seen before, and I am unacquainted with his name.'

'Oh!' rejoined the old sailor, 'I am sure I know him; it must be my good St. Joseph, who has at last heard the three Paters and Aves, which from my childhood I have offered to him to obtain the grace of a happy death.'

And then for a last time he recited in thanksgiving those saving prayers, which had opened to him the arms of the Divine mercy, and later obtained, we may hope, that the gates of Paradise should be thrown open to receive him.

For he died, as truly all the faithful clients of St. Joseph may hope to die, with the smile of peace upon his lips, and joy and confidence in his heart.

11. St. Joseph and a Freemason.

We take the following account of a wonderful grace obtained by the intercession of St. Joseph, from the relation of the Carmelite Father Philip, of St. Bernard, and which appeared in a paper, entitled, 'The Devout Client of St. Joseph.'

'Having heard that a young man from Cologna, in the diocese of Ravenna, who had unfortunately fallen into the snares of the Freemasons, had obtained a singular grace from St. Joseph, the patron of the Universal Church, I asked the parish priest of that place to give me an exact account of all the circumstances of the event, my intention being to publish them in this periodical, that thereby the powerful influence of the Saint might become more and more renowned , and that the faithful might be more excited to have recourse to him in all their necessities, and acquire the strong conviction of that saying of St. Teresa, the great promoter of this devotion, "that it is granted to St. Joseph to afford help in every need, whereas the other Saints only bring help in some particular necessity."

'The following is the letter which I received from the parish priest in answer to my request.

' "REVEREND FATHER,

' "Your Reverence has inquired about the particular circumstances concerning a certain apothecary of this place called Gabriel Cassini, whose death occurred on April 10th, 1868.

' "I most willingly comply with your desire as this event is likely to show forth the mercy of God, and the powerful intercession of the glorious St. Joseph; perhaps also some sinful soul may be touched by this account, and return to the way of salvation.

' "Gabriel Cassini, a young man of about thirty-three years of age, was when thus in the prime of life, seized by a slow, but mortal disease. Towards the end of the year 1867, his state of health grew so much worse as to become hopeless. Although his end was evidently approaching, he still so clung to life that he would not hear of the necessity of attending to the concerns of his soul. I feared, therefore, that he would die without receiving the Sacraments of the Church. On Christmas morning I received intelligence that his illness had so much increased that he was hardly expected to live for more than a few hours. Nevertheless, he expressed no desire to see a priest, but showed a determined unwillingness to admit one. I was in the greatest perplexity, as I feared to make matters worse if I presented myself unsought.

' "Then I felt inspired to offer the third Mass of Christmas for the dying man with the intention that God in His mercy would check the progress of the disease, in order to give him time to apply himself to the care of his eternal salvation. Before the close of the day I was filled with an indescribable consolation and hope on receiving the information that a great change for the better had come over the sick man. I waited a few days, and then under the pretence of a visit, I tried to come into communication with him, and when he received me, I found him strong enough to be able to converse a little without over-fatigue. Then as I saw that my visit seemed to give him pleasure, I resolved to call again, but for the sake of preparing the way, I kept the conversation upon indifferent topics, so that by degrees I might the better bring forward the important subjects about which I wanted to treat with him, whenever an opportunity should present itself.

' "He went on as usual for about a month, when suddenly he was again taken so ill that great apprehensions were felt of his approaching end. I did not cease to call, and awaited the opportunity of speaking to him about his soul. On the 10th of March, the first day of St. Joseph's Novena, he spoke with sadness, lamenting that his life was ebbing slowly but surely away. The moment seemed to have come to broach the subject that was so near my heart, and I said as gently and kindly as I could:

' "Sir, if indeed you feel weaker, you should think a little of your soul."

' "Hardly had I uttered these words than he fixed his eyes glaringly upon me as if wishing to intimidate me and exclaimed:

' "I suspected indeed that your frequent visits had some particular aim, but you must know that I will hear nothing about the Pope, the priests, or confession, and that I shall never give in to any of your nonsensical delusions."

' "My dear friend, I replied in the mildest tone I could command, your illness has become so serious that I cannot enter into a discussion with you without risk of accelerating your death, and thus depriving you of these last precious moments, which you ought to employ in reflecting upon your salvation; but one thing I may tell you, and that is, many stronger minds than yours, who were like you, enemies to Religion, have, in such moments as these altered their opinions, and on the brink of eternity renounced their foolish prejudices. Consider well, if you love your soul, that you be not deceived, for such an error will be irreparable. Now I will go, for fear I should disquiet you and make you worse, but I shall pray for you as I did before. On Christmas night when you were in a similar crisis, I offered the third Mass with the intention that God in His Mercy would grant you time for conversion. Now I will pray with all confidence that God in His Goodness will bestow on you the treasures of His infinite compassion. May the blessing of the Lord come upon you!"

' "With tears in my eyes I left the house, and coming home I began at once a Novena to St. Joseph. Shortly afterwards I heard again that the sick man's state was getting worse, but that my words had seemed to make a deep impression upon him; he suffered from violent convulsions and a burning fever that deprived him of all rest at night and left him no peace. All these alarming symptoms suddenly ceased on the feast of St. Joseph, when towards evening he was heard to exclaim:

' "O priest! thou hast done for me! since thy visit I can find no peace!'

' "His parents on hearing this, endeavoured to quiet him, and said:

' "The priest has but done his duty, and sought to do you good. Never has a member of our family died without receiving the last Sacraments. Do you want to be the first, and cause that greatest of sorrows to your parents? To-day is the feast of St. Joseph, the Patron and Protector of all at the hour of death; invoke him fervently and he will give you peace.'

' "No sooner were these words spoken than he said:

' "Ask the parish priest to send me early to-morrow morning Father Pietro Casoni (the priest of Berra, a neighbouring priest); I will make my confession to him, and then you must try and be at peace with me; who knows but that we shall all agree and be satisfied.'

' "Not a moment's delay was made in communicating to me this consoling news, although it was already late at night. The next morning with all speed I sent word to Father Pietro Casoni that he was wanted, and he, full of zeal for the salvation of a soul, came to me without delay.

' "Then we agreed as to what should be required from the young man in order that his conversion might be clearly proved, namely to renounce his error, and to give up the books, that he had published against Faith and Religion. He refused nothing that was demanded of him, but rather gave in to all most willingly without suggesting any, even the least, condition. After receiving the Holy Sacraments he never ceased expressing his satisfaction to all present, showing himself truly penitent for his errors, and asking pardon of all. He desired also to see me again to retract what he had said when I first attempted to mention the subject of his conversion, he then asked me to send him a priest who would stay with him to the last. I kissed him on the forehead and we parted, mutually happy and content.

' "I sent my chaplain to assist him, and every day, even several times a day he renewed his confession, until the Friday of the following week, which was Good Friday, when he peacefully gave up his soul to his Creator, about seven o'clock in the morning.

' "I forgot to mention that on Palm Sunday, on which day the Paschal time begins, he desired that Holy Communion should be brought to him in a very solemn and public manner, that he might endeavour thereby to make atonement and reparation for the scandal he had given by his impiety.

' "Such, Reverend Father, is the exact account, of the illness, conversion, and death of the person whose history you have asked me to relate to you.

' "FRANCESKO PASINI, Archpriest.
' "COLOGNA, *July* 27, 1828.' "

12. THE APOSTOLATE OF PRAYER.

In the Hospital of the Red Cross at Lyons there lived an old soldier who professed no religion whatever—we might call him an atheist without being far wrong. But how came this unfortunate man to be so utterly incredulous? Alas, it was the fruit of a bad education. He was born at the time of the French Revolution, when people were so insensate as to try to do away with the worship of God; when the churches were shut up, and the priests were murdered or exiled. Thus the poor man had grown up without knowledge of religion; indeed, he was utterly ignorant of the truths of Faith. He had been a soldier, and served under Emperor Napoleon in the war against Spain, during which he, like most of his fellow soldiers, became guilty of many sacrileges, having robbed and desecrated the churches, and committed many other crimes.

Now, he could not bear to hear mention made of a priest, or of a confessor, or the performance of any religious duty, and he had an especial aversion to members of any religious order.

But God in His mercy had given him a daughter who was exceedingly good and pious. This loving child had for a long time been secretly sighing and praying for her unhappy father whose soul was in so pitiful a state. Not a day passed in which she did not beseech Almighty God to save the soul of her dear parent, and bring him back to the faith.

In her humility she could not trust to the efficacy of her own prayers, she besought all the pious souls she knew to unite with her in her fervent supplications for the conversion of her father.

One day a devoted client of St. Joseph, to whom this good daughter had confided her trouble, had the good inspiration to send several little books concerning the devotion to the Seven Joys and Sorrows of St. Joseph to the Sisters of Mercy who attended the hospital in which the old soldier was.

This charitable soul requested that they would unite in the devotion of the Seven Sundays to obtain the conversion of the unhappy father. Meanwhile the pious daughter redoubled her fervent supplications. At last God was moved by her persevering constancy. The man who formerly was inaccessible to any religious influence was suddenly softened.

The grace of God had touched him, and light had shone in his soul.

He had lived forty-five years without approaching the Sacraments. Now he confessed his sins with marks of great contrition, and his daughter had the consolation of receiving Holy Communion with him on the Friday in Passion Week, 1862.

From that day forward he was a changed man, and his daughter never ceased extolling the power and goodness of St. Joseph.

Learn from this good daughter, my dear children, to pray also with fervour for your parents when they are in any spiritual or temporal need. The love you owe them makes this a duty incumbent on you.

13. PROTECTION IN THE HOUR OF DEATH.

The devotion to St. Joseph, the Foster-Father of our Redeemer, spreads ever more and more throughout the world. It is as if this humble Saint had been forced, as it were, to step out of his obscurity to reveal to all Christians the greatness of his intercessory power.

And what marvel is it that he has such power? When we think of all he did for Jesus during his life on earth, is it any wonder that Jesus attends now to his prayers?

The incident we are about to relate is only one more example to prove how faithfully St. Joseph bestows graces on his clients.

A French missionary writes:

'I was riding one day wearily along the sandy banks of the Senegal, in Africa, on a route completely unknown to me. The serpents slid away hissing into the grass, the crocodiles went plunging into the swamps, the sun's burning rays poured fiercely down. An invisible power seemed to urge me forward. At length I came in sight of a hut. I dismounted, and was about to push open the door, when a voice from within cried out excitedly:

' "Who's there?"

' "A Father Missioner," I answered; "don't be alarmed. May the peace of God rest on this dwelling."

' "A priest! exclaimed the stranger, in good French. "You are most welcome. Lose no time, but come to me immediately."

' "Who are you, then? and how do you come to lie here?"

' "As these questions can wait, my Father, let me simply tell you that I am down with my third attack of fever, and that it will be my last, as you well know. Let us defer talking of other matters till later. I will answer your questions should I survive. But I am quite prepared for confession, so please, Father, let us begin at once."

'As he spoke I heard the howl of some jackals, allured as they ever are by the scent of death. I felt convinced by their approach that the sick man had not long to live, and proceeded to administer the last Sacraments without delay.

'I now felt persuaded that the invisible power that had urged me on was of Almighty God, and in order that I might understand His ways the better, I said to the dying man:

' "You must surely have prayed very earnestly that God would send you a priest, for evidently it was your Guardian Angel that brought me here.'

' "Would you like to know how it came to pass?"

' "Certainly."

' "I felt sure a priest would come."

' "But how so, nothing, humanly speaking, was more unlikely than that one would come into this wild desert of Africa?"

' "Oh, but human probability had nothing to do with it. I always wear the cord of St. Joseph, and I belong to the Confraternity of the 'Bona Mors.' You see, my conscience was in a bad state, so St. Joseph was obliged to send me a priest. I recommended the matter to him most earnestly, and, as you can bear witness, not in vain."

' "Now all is clear to me," I answered. "Keep still your confidence in St. Joseph. Death is approaching; but death, when you can invoke the holy Names of Jesus, Mary, and Joseph, only ushers you into their presence."

'The fever raged on, and within two hours from the time I entered the hut the man was dead.'

14. How Sweet it is to Die with St. Joseph as our Guardian.

Many saints have said, and it is most true, that at the hour of death, our Lord shields with His special protection the souls of such as have in life shown themselves compassionate and merciful, and have bestowed protection upon Him, in the persons of His poor, suffering members in that hour of extremity.

Not very long ago a retired major of the French army died without any agony, under the guardianship of St. Joseph, after a long and painful illness, which he had borne with exemplary patience.

M. François F— —, of Annecy, who had raised himself by his talents to the rank of major in the Savoyard regiment, had, when not engaged in actual warfare, a far more difficult enemy to gain the mastery over, than any he was likely to meet on the field of battle. His own eager impetuous nature was a thousand times more dangerous to him, and more difficult to conquer, than any mortal foe. Therefore it was that Almighty God, who had for him special designs of mercy, visited him with a paralysis that necessitated his passing ten years in an arm-chair. This must have been in order to oblige this officer, naturally so active and energetic, to lead a quiet and retired life; for in consequence of his affliction he was compelled to withdraw from the army. He then took up his residence on an estate belonging to him, which was situated on the banks of the Lake of Annecy.

Here he divided his time between reading good books, and saying his Rosary. In order to pass the time away, he used to get his servants to wheel his chair every day into a little alcove which had been made close to the principal street of the village, where of an afternoon he often sat beneath the shade of the trees to receive the visits of his friends.

On one side of this spot stood a beautiful statue of the Immaculate Conception, and on the other side one of Our Lady's Virginal Spouse, St. Joseph. Here he would frequently read the 'Annals of the Propagation,' the touching incidents recorded in which often brought the tears into his eyes.

If he happened to see a weary traveller or a peasant, exhausted with his labours, passing along the road, he would always send his servant to bring them some refreshment.

But time would fail to recount all the acts of charity which love for his neighbour inspired him to fulfill. So let it suffice to say that despite being possessed of a military outspokenness, which made it impossible for him ever to dissemble or refrain from the frank expression of his thoughts, he had not a single enemy.

To compensate this excellent man for his many afflictions, God had given him a wife who was a perfect model of cheerful self-denial and willing mortification, and a daughter also most amiable, and possessed of a solid piety. These two devoted their lives to nursing him, and were to him like consoling angels; their tender and exquisite love assuaged his sorrows, so that he scarcely thought of his sufferings.

It is to his daughter's pen that we owe the following account of his last moments:

'All is over; this morning my dear father rendered up his purified soul unto God, after thirty-five years of exquisite suffering, which he bore with exemplary patience. Shortly before his death he said to me:

' "It seems as if St. Joseph would have me wait for his month before calling me hence. Well, it is a long time, but God's Will be done."

'Seeing that death was rapidly approaching, I said to him:

' "Dear father, I think that St. Joseph, loving you so very much as he does, wishes to have you with him sooner than that."

'At this his face lit up with an expression of indescribable joy, and he exclaimed:

' "Oh, my child, if only it may be so; if only God will graciously hear our prayers that it may be so."

'He requested once again to receive Holy Communion. He then asked me to place a picture of St. Joseph at the foot of his bed, so that he might have it constantly before his eyes. A few hours before his death he desired to go to confession, in order to gain the indulgence of the confraternity of the "Bona Mors."

' "My child," he said to me, "I am now in the death-struggle; I can no longer pray for myself. Do you pray for me."

'We all knelt around his bed and prayed for some time, and seeing that his dying eyes still sought to look at the picture of St. Joseph, I held it nearer to him.

'With his Crucifix in one hand, and his Rosary of Our Lady of Lourdes in the other, he continued to make the sign of the Cross from time to time, and then, with one last look at St. Joseph, he gently breathed his last. His face became quite transformed, his features expressed such peace of soul as it is impossible to describe.

'Our Lady obtained for him the grace to die on a Saturday to reward him for the many Rosaries he had said in her honour during his long sleepless nights.'

15. Conversion of a Great Sinner through the Intercession of St. Joseph.

A Sister of Charity, who places all her confidence in St. Joseph, has communicated the following account to us. It will serve as one more proof of the salvation of a soul, the care of which we have committed to Mary and Joseph:

A lady, who not only had lost the faith, but who prided herself on being an atheist, and who seemed to delight in uttering the most frightful blasphemies against God, His priests, and the Church at large, was at length attacked by a severe and dangerous illness, and lay sick for a long time. Only the year before she was seized with this illness, she dismissed a person from her house merely because she ventured to suggest that she should provide that her niece, who was dying of cholera, might receive the last Sacraments.

Yet, notwithstanding the malignity of her perversity, Almighty God looked upon this unfortunate soul with an eye of pity and compassion; and He permitted that a train of circumstances should wonderfully unite to bring about the conversion of this hardened sinner.

In the first place she became acquainted almost accidentally with a lady called Philomena, who was, although the invalid was unaware of it, a devoted client of St. Joseph. But what could be effected in such a case of openly professed unbelief and impiety? Nothing could be done, in the first instance, but to pray to St. Joseph, and to place unbounded confidence in his paternal care and pity, and in this verily lies the art of working miracles.

But Philomena not only prayed; she was assiduous in paying visits to the sick lady, and not less assiduous in endeavouring, by the help of St. Joseph to season her conversations with wisdom, and to lose no opportunity of introducing subjects calculated to lead to the conversion she had so much at heart.

'Prayer!' ejaculated the invalid one day, 'do not talk to me of prayer! I know no longer what it is to pray. Why, I do not remember a single word of any of the prayers I learnt when I was young.'

'Then, my dear friend,' interposed Philomena, 'suppose you begin to learn some new ones now you are old. Join me in saying a beautiful little prayer, which we will offer for the recovery of your health,' and she began to recite the 'Memorare.'

She was immediately interrupted by an exclamation of:

'Oh, I remember often having said that when I was a child!' and the lady joined with her lips, if not with her heart, in all the words of that most efficacious prayer.

This was a great step gained, and Philomena redoubled the fervour of her intercessions, and that with increased confidence. But the alarming nature of the illness increased daily. At last one day, with fear and trembling, this true friend broached the subject of confession, and this elicited at once a scene of violence. The invalid stormed vehemently against the very idea of such a thing, and protested again and again 'that never, never, never should a priest gain admittance into her house.'

What was to be done?

Oh, good St. Joseph! Is all our confidence in you to prove in vain! Will you for the first time turn a deaf ear to our supplications? But no; that can never come to pass. We must pray harder, and instead of letting discouragement cause us to relax our efforts we must set to work more vigorously than ever.

The next time Philomena called, she brought with her a pretty picture of St. Joseph, the patron of the dying, and as she presented it to her friend, she said:

'See, you are suffering so much; you should fasten this picture to your bed and you will be sure to obtain relief if you will say for nine days, "St. Joseph, pray for me." '

To Philomena's great delight, the invalid readily agreed to do this, and in her joy at beholding her once more about to pray, she could not but believe that her conversion must be near at hand. This kind friend then went at once to an institution for children, which was dedicated to St. Joseph, and obtained that a Novena should be made for the sick lady.

But what was to be done about confession? She felt it perfectly impossible that she could ever again approach the subject to her, after the hot outburst of indignation it had before elicited.

'St. Joseph, I leave that to you,' she said. 'I can venture nothing further in that matter.'

Meanwhile the Novena was commenced by the children, and the invalid was as good as her word, she daily invoked St. Joseph, and when she was well enough she said the prayer, which was printed under the picture.

Now came the second link in the chain of Providence. A good woman from Brittany was sent for to nurse and give some special assistance that was required, and this good creature, devoid of all education or learning, but full of faith and unfeigned simplicity, was the instrument chosen by St. Joseph for the carrying out of his designs.

By degrees she began quite naturally to speak to her patient of the Sacrament of Penance, saying how happy she would be when she had made a good confession, and lamenting over the wickedness of those poor people who hate the priests, without knowing anything about them. At last she begged the lady to allow a priest to come and see her.

The lady seemed almost to hesitate, but the evil spirit did not fail to put an obstacle in the way.

'What would people say,' she said, 'to see a priest coming to visit me after my having declared for so many years that a religious man should never cross my threshold?'

But the good Bretonne answered in her candid simplicity:

'The neighbours will only say, "Well, this lady has at least too good a heart to die like a dog!"'

The last day of the Novena had dawned, Philomena was directing her steps towards the house of the invalid, turning over in her mind one last effort she would try to make, when suddenly she met the sick nurse on her way to tell her the joyful tidings, that the patient had herself asked for a priest, and had received all the last Sacraments with wonderful devotion.

At first Philomena thought it must be a dream; then she flew to the bedside of her friend, who embraced her whilst shedding a flood of tears.

'Oh, how miserable I have been!' she exclaimed; 'I maintained that there was no God, Who governs us all, and now this good God, Whom I have so entirely forgotten and neglected, and so grievously offended, forgives me everything. What a grace! and dear St. Joseph, whose picture I treasure, has obtained it for me. I was so impious, so unbelieving, oh! that I could prolong my life that I might make reparation for the past, but God in His mercy will arrange it all.'

Two days later, she yielded up her soul into the hands of Him Who, by the intercession of St. Joseph, had dealt so mercifully with her.

The children who had made the Novena, were so overjoyed at the news of this conversion, which was nothing short of a miracle of grace, that, in their gratitude, they began at once another Novena of Thanksgiving to St. Joseph. This is the real way to obtain fresh favours.

16. St. Joseph softens a Hard Heart.

In the year 1876 Mr. N——of Marseilles, became dangerously ill, the anxiety of his relations was very great, not only on account of his great age, of over eighty-two years, which left little hope of any but a fatal termination to his illness, but also because he had lived, for the last sixty years, without any professions of religion, and in open, and persistent neglect of all the practices enjoined by Holy Church.

How much, and how frequently his family prayed for the beloved, but unhappy man, no one can ever tell. How many tears were shed over him by his wife and children, who alike deplored his delusion; but all in vain.

Meanwhile his pious wife had died, without having had the consolation of witnessing his conversion; and shortly after his death, his eldest daughter, who had an especially tender love for her father, entered a religious order, in obedience to an interior inspiration, which moved her to offer herself as a living sacrifice, to Almighty God, hoping by this means to obtain for her beloved parent the grace of conversion.

It was but a few months after she had entered the Convent, and whilst she was, as a fervent Novice, devoting herself to the duties of her Vocation, that her father was seized with this alarming illness.

His friends, as well as his relations, tried every means they could think of, to persuade him to seek reconciliation with God, but in vain.

'Let me alone,' he always replied; 'I will have nothing to do with a religion, that has deprived me of my dearest daughter.'

To everyone's astonishment, he rallied, and recovered from this first attack, but he only continued to lead, as before, a life of utter worldliness and estrangement from God.

Soon, however, the hand of the Lord again struck him down, and towards the end of February, a severe relapse into the same illness caused the greatest apprehensions to be entertained for his life.

An excellent priest was summoned, and brought to his bedside by his sorrowful, and anxious relations, but the sick man would enter into no conversation with him, and he had to leave without having accomplished any good, and when a few days later he attempted to renew his visit, he was flatly refused admittance.

At these distressing occurrences, the anxiety of his children became greater than ever, each of them tried to storm the hard heart, and soften their father by their love and tears but all were equally unsuccessful.

One day, his second daughter who was married, said to him:

'Oh my dear father, you know how much we all love you, and how grateful we are for all the good things we have received from you during the course of our lives; but equally great is our distress now, at your refusing every consolation of our holy religion. We all hope one day to enter heaven, where our dear mother already awaits us; will you alone separate yourself from us for all eternity! Oh no, dear father; you surely will not, cannot do so!'

But the dying man remained obdurate and hardened, every appeal was unavailing. The parish priest came, and spoke to him of the love, and mercy of the Crucified, but when he held the Crucifix before him Mr. N——pushed it aside with violence. There seemed no hope, but in prayer. Day and night intercession was made for his conversion. St. Joseph, the great patron of the dying, was especially invoked, and a vow was offered, in case he should grant their prayer.

In order to leave no stone unturned, and nothing undone that could possibly soften the hard heart, the thought occurred to them to obtain permission that the eldest daughter might be allowed to come and assist her father in his last moments.

The leave of her ecclesiastical superiors was sought, and obtained, so the young Novice, in holy obedience, left her cloister at once; and the next morning, humbly, and quietly took her place at the bedside of her dying parent.

Astonished and surprised, he at first regarded her with a look of cold indifference, but by-and-by it changed, and softened into a look of loving sorrow. The hard heart could not withstand the mild entreating looks, and words, of one whose love for him had caused her to offer up her life in sacrifice for him.

Grace at last triumphed completely! His determined resistance broke down before the force of this great love. A few hours later, and he who had so recently scoffed at the very mention of prayer, joyfully acceded to the proposal that the Rosary should be recited at his bedside.

All his children, and every member of the household gathered round, and joined in praying and conjuring the Spouse of Mary to accomplish his work to the end. For all felt that this had been brought about through the intercession of St. Joseph.

The Rosary finished, the good priest was again summoned, and this time his offers were willingly and gratefully accepted.

They left him alone with the dying man, who with every mark of true contrition made a humble confession of his whole life, and with touching devotion received the Sacrament of Extreme Unction. Holy Communion he was not able to receive, as he was unable to swallow. He lingered still for some days in unspeakable suffering, which he bore not only with patience, but also with gratitude.

'Oh, but I am happy now,' he used to say, even when the pain was at its height, 'very happy.' And as often as the priest held the Crucifix before him, he would press it with joyful love to his poor white lips, with the hands which only a few days before had thrust it from him.

It had now come to the 25th of March, the Feast of the Annunciation, and about midnight as his children were all kneeling around his bed, the old man entered upon his agony. Once more he turned his eyes, already dim, upon the Crucifix, and then upon his kneeling children, as if to say farewell, and then his spirit sped into the presence of his Creator.

His children at length arose from their knees, with hearts full of consolation and overflowing with gratitude to St. Joseph, for the miracle of love that he had wrought, in obtaining for their father so happy a death.

In conclusion let me say, if you wish to afford a special pleasure to St. Joseph, ask him by fervent prayer to help you to pluck out and destroy the very roots of sin from your heart, and if, as may be the case, you have someone on earth who is dear to you, and for whom you have already prayed for a long, long time, that he might turn from the path of sin, and as yet seemingly all in vain, do not be discouraged. Go with confidence to St. Joseph, he knows what it is to lose God.

He once lost his Foster-Child, the Son of God, and sought for Him for three days with unspeakable anguish of heart. And so he ever has compassion upon these secret griefs, and understands and sympathizes with them.

Call upon him urgently then, to help you to seek the soul that is lost to you, as he sought for the Holy Child Jesus, as indefatigably, as steadfastly, so that you may find it to all eternity happy in Heaven.

17. OUT OF MY DIARY.

The following occurrence is one more evidence of the fact that St. Joseph may truly be called the Patron of the Dying.

The priest of the parish of Notre Dame in Munster, Westphalia, was called one night to go to a man who was dying. The house in which the sick man lay was clearly described to him, and he hastened thither with all speed. But the inmates of the house seemed all wrapped in profound slumber. He rang and rang the bell, and at length the door was opened, but in answer to his request to be led to the sick man who had sent for him, he was told that there was no one ill in that house, it must be some mistake.

The priest could only shake his head and go on again wonderingly. Scarcely had he reached his house before he was again summoned, and by the same man, to go to the same house.

'But I have but this moment returned from that house,' said the priest, 'and they say there is no sick person there.'

'And notwithstanding what they said, there is,' replied the unknown; 'an old man is dying in a room quite at the top of the house.'

The priest at once retraced his steps, and when he came to the house he asked the man who opened the door if there was not someone living in the attic under the roof.

'Yes,' he answered, 'an old man lives up there; but I am not aware that he is ill, he has always appeared in very good health.'

The priest asked to be allowed to go up and see him. And he found the old man ill, very ill, and nearly dying. But he had always besought St. Joseph to be near him, in his last conflict;

and he had not asked in vain. He was now able to receive all the last Sacraments, and before morning he was dead.

Who was the man who had twice called the priest?

18. The Picture of St. Joseph's Death.

In the large and populous town of X——lived a rich gentleman, who had spent the greater part of his life in pursuit of the pleasures and luxuries of this world, without religion or thought or care for God.

But now when old, a grievous and lingering disease laid hold of him. He had been baptized and brought up as a Catholic, but it was in vain that his pious wife, or the venerable priest whom she had called to her assistance, pleaded with him to return to his duties. He only laughed at them, and all their endeavours were ineffectual, to soften the hard and flinty heart of the poor sinner.

One day a young and very simply-dressed woman came to the house, bringing with her a picture which she wished to sell. She told them that her husband was an artist, but that for some months past he had been obliged to give up painting since he was suffering from an affection of the nerves which rendered him unable to pursue his art. This calamity had reduced their circumstances to such an extent that they felt obliged to try to sell the picture she had brought, which nothing but so great a misfortune would have induced them to part with.

She further added that she came to offer it first to Mr. N—— because they had heard that he was a great connoisseur, and rich.

At these words she uncovered the picture, and behold, it was St. Joseph lying on his death-bed, and beside him the

Blessed Virgin, his Spouse, and her Divine Son!

It was exquisitely delineated, and Mr. N——and his wife were equally charmed with the painting. They soon agreed about the price, and Mr. N——had the picture hung up on the wall opposite his bed, that he might delight his eyes with the contemplation of the beautiful representation of the holy scene. And as his eyes constantly rested upon what was so touchingly portrayed, it seemed as if his heart opened to Divine grace, and softened more and more.

Only the next day he said to his wife:

'I have a presentiment that my end is approaching—if only I could die like St. Joseph, with Jesus and Mary beside me.'

His wife endeavoured to suppress her weeping as she replied:

'Oh, Victorin, receive the Holy Sacraments, and then death, which I pray God may not come to you yet for many years, would become easy, nay, sweet to you, through the intercession of the holy ones you see in that picture.'

'Do you really think so, Anna?' began the sick man dubiously. 'St. Joseph can know nothing about rancour and ill-will. What would he have to say to me, when I have banished our only son Ferdinand from my house, and from my heart, since he offended me by his marriage? When that poor painter's wife brought the picture to be sold the other day, I could not help thinking to myself, my son Ferdinand also is a painter; perhaps he also may be in distress or poverty, but he finds no assistance or help from me. For years past I have left his letters unopened and unanswered.'

'Thy son Ferdinand,' rejoined his wife, with difficulty forcing back her tears, 'has been for the last fortnight living in this town; he has been in great poverty and distress, but he has refused to accept assistance from me since I could not give it without keeping you in ignorance of it. The price, however, which his wife received from you for his picture has preserved them from destitution.'

'What!' exclaimed Victorin, 'my son here, in this very town! And that was his wife whom I saw. Oh, my God! I thank Thee!' he added in a trembling voice.'

'Shall I then send to fetch our son?' exclaimed his wife instantly.

'Do so, Anna,' replied her husband, 'and tell him that his father's heart is longing after a reconciliation with him, and that I wish to learn to know his wife. But bid them not to come till to-morrow, for first, before all else, I must seek to make my peace with God. I can offer my Redeemer my broken and contrite heart, and endeavour to obtain the expiation of my sins by a penitent confession and fervent Communion.'

He received the last Sacraments with earnest devotion that day.

And on the morrow the meeting of reconciliation took place between the parents and the son they had not seen for so many years. No words can describe what that meeting was, nor the introduction of the wife and children, unknown till now.

'My son,' said Victorin, with tears in his eyes, 'it is to your rare genius that I owe both my reconciliation to God, to you, and your family.'

'Do not say that, dear father,' broke in Ferdinand, 'after God, we owe all the happiness of this hour to St. Joseph. To his protection and intercession I have every day committed myself, my parents, my wife and children, and the success of the feeble efforts of my pencil.'

A few days later, and Victorin, surrounded by his wife, his

son, and all his family, departed this life. With his last breath he uttered the holy Names of 'Jesus, Mary, Joseph.'

V.
St. Joseph our helper in Every Variety of Necessity.

1. Venerate St. Joseph if You Wish to Die Happily.

A Venetian merchant had the habit of daily visiting an image of St. Joseph which stood in a niche at the corner of one of the streets of the town in which he lived.

Falling sick of a dangerous illness, which soon brought him to the brink of the grave, St. Joseph appeared to him as his last moments approached. At the sight of the Saint, towards whom he had ever been so devout, the sick man was filled with consolation, but above all his conscience became so enlightened, that in an instant he seemed to perceive clearly all the sins of his past life, and in their full heinousness and guilt; while at the same time he felt a new and exceeding great contrition, together with the sweetest hope of pardon.

As a priest was present with him, he made a fresh and fervent confession, and having received absolution, full of peace and joy, piously expired in our Lord.

2. Mary and Joseph.

The venerable servant of God, Alexis of Vigevano, a Capuchin, ended his meritorious life with a death full of sweetness.

A few moments before his departure he asked one of the

brothers to light some candles. They were astonished at his request, and wanted to know the reason of it.

'Our dear Lady is coming presently with her Spouse, and therefore it is fitting to light candles, that they may both be received with the greatest reverence.'

Soon they perceived that the visit he had predicted had already come to pass, for the dying Father exclaimed, radiant with joy:

'There comes the Queen of Heaven! There comes St. Joseph! Kneel down, my brethren, to receive them reverently.'

But he was now to reap the fruits of this heavenly visitation, for at the same moment, in the presence of Mary and Joseph, he breathed out his soul into their hands.

It was the 19th of March, the day of triumph for St. Joseph, who visited this good religious on his feast day, to reward him for the loving devotion he had always shown to him.

3. St. Joseph, Teacher of Prayer.

Prayer and meditation are the food of interior life. Therefore we should beseech St. Joseph that he may obtain for us the grace to be very faithful in these two practices, and that we may perform them in a right manner.

Saint Teresa says:

'Let him who needs a guide to lead him on in the way of prayer and meditation take St. Joseph as a master, for he will show him the right path, and safely conduct him to a good termination.'

Father Barry relates:

'A religious desired once, as she herself confessed to me, to be freed from her distractions in prayer. In order to obtain this grace, she felt herself inspired to have recourse to St. Joseph. She did so with great devotion, and the gift of prayer was bestowed on her in a high measure.'

4. FATHER PICOT DE CLORIVIÈRE.

This saintly priest was a member of the congregation of the Sacred Heart in the time of the terrible French Revolution. It seems that he had obtained from St. Joseph the grace of an ever-increasing love to the most Holy Sacrament of the Altar. Against all expectation, he was ordained priest; but he had so great an impediment in his speech, that he would have been unable to give himself to the apostolic labours if he had not been cured of this defect in a miraculous manner. Then he preached in many churches, and as his only reward, he desired to obtain through the intercession of St. Joseph from God the grace to die at the foot of the Altar in adoration of the most Holy Sacrament, without being a burden to anyone. St. Joseph who is so powerful over the Heart of Jesus, certainly pleaded for the request of his client. For one Sunday, when, as usual, Father Picot de Clorivière went to the chapel in order to pay a visit to Our Lord in the Blessed Sacrament. He knelt down, and as his weakness did not allow of his kneeling upright without support, he leant his elbow on a railing which separated the sanctuary from the church. Then he began to pray; but his soul followed his prayer, and ascended also on high before the Throne of God. One of the Fathers, who had just before heard his confession and given him absolution, was witness of this holy death. He died at the age of eighty-five years.

5. St. Joseph a Guide on the Road.

A pious lay-brother of the great Benedictine monastery of Monserrat in Spain, had the custom of venerating with particular devotion the mystery of the Flight into Egypt.

His heart especially grieved at all St. Joseph had to suffer, when he had to fly in such great poverty and haste, with Jesus and Mary, into a strange and idolatrous country. It once happened that this brother had to return to his monastery from a great distance. Already the shadows of evening were falling, it began to grow dark, and the monastery was still far off. Suddenly he perceived that he had lost his way, and he feared that he should have to spend the night in the open air, surrounded by dangerous precipices; and it was the more sad as, to the dangers of the mountains, was added the fear of the wild beasts, which he knew infested those parts.

All of a sudden, whilst he was full of those anxious thoughts, he saw not far off a man, who led a donkey by a bridle. Seated on its back was a lady of exceedingly great beauty, with a most noble and majestic appearance. In her arms rested a little sleeping child. The Brother hastened forward to meet the stranger in order to ask him to direct him in the right way. But his joy at this sight increased still more, and was mixed with sweet consolation, as the unknown man bade him follow him, and promised to guide him to the monastery.

Whilst they pursued their way, conversations of wonderful unction refreshed the heart of the Brother; but scarcely was the monastery gate in view, than suddenly the guide and his family disappeared from before his eyes, and nowhere was the least trace of them to be discovered. But in the heart of the

Brother awoke the joyful conviction that St. Joseph himself had been his guide, and that he had rewarded in this manner his devotion to his sorrow, in the mystery of the Flight into Egypt.

6. A Beautiful Death of a Faithful Client of St. Joseph.

The venerable Franciscan Nun, Prudentia Zagnoni, who was renowned for her extraordinary virtues, had during her whole life a most fervent devotion to St. Joseph. In return, at her death she received an exceeding great favour; for the Saint appeared to her and assisted her in her agony. In order to give her still more consolation, he held in his arms Him Who is the joy of the Angels, the Divine Child Jesus.

The good nun drew from this sight the sweetest consolation and delight; her joy was not to be described, and the nuns who were present assisting at her agony were much touched as they heard her conversing now with St. Joseph and now with the Divine Child, thanking them for their visit, and declaring that she already tasted beforehand the joys of Paradise.

From her looks and gestures, it was evident to all around that St. Joseph had given her the Divine Child to caress in her arms, thus giving to his faithful servant the highest proof of his favour that he was able in the moment of her greatest need and extremity.

7. St. Joseph a Master of the Interior Life.

A Father of the Society of Jesus, being on a journey, met one day a young man with whom he entered into conversation. He very soon recognised in him a chosen soul, rich in graces and rare gifts, so that he could not remember ever to have found a soul more advanced in perfection.

But his astonishment increased as he learned that no one had ever instructed the young man concerning the lessons of a spiritual life; yet he heard him speaking on the most sublime subjects like a saint and a theologian. As the Father could not understand how this could be, he asked the young man where he had gained this wisdom and spiritual knowledge.

'Ten years ago,' he replied, 'God inspired me to choose St. Joseph for my patron saint and guide; all that I have learnt has been from him.'

Then he spoke of the sanctity of the Foster-Father of Jesus, and concluded his conversation with the assurance that this Saint was the special guide and protector of those souls, who led a hidden and interior life.

8. How St. Joseph rewards those who Promote his Honour.

When Father Lallemant was Rector of the Jesuit College at Bourges, he called two of the young professors and promised each of them that they should receive that grace which they most desired, if they would exhort their scholars to venerate St. Joseph, and offer him some particular homage on his feast, which was just then approaching. The two professors joyfully agreed to this proposal, and they so zealously encouraged their scholars that on the feast of St. Joseph both classes received Holy Communion in his honour, besides performing other practices of devotion.

On the same day, the two professors went to the Father-Rector, and revealed to him secretly the particular grace which they were each desirous to receive. The first was the celebrated Fr. Nouet, who desired the grace to be able to write and to speak worthily of our Divine Saviour. It is not known what grace the second asked for, but it is known for certain that he, as well as Fr. Nouet, obtained what he desired.

Verses on St. Joseph.

IN a silent, lonely workshop
An old man is toiling away,
He works ever harder and harder,
The whole of the livelong day.
Great drops stand out on his forehead,
Which is lined with anxious care,
And trickle slowly downward,
Through the locks of his silvery hair.

But see! for a moment he raises
His noble, but oft-bowed head;
And a look of radiant gladness,
Makes bright the lowly shed.
Peace seems to reign around him,
A serene and heavenly peace,—
Yet he grasps his plane more tightly,
For the work, that he must not cease.

'Work on, work on, unweariedly,
Oh! arms, put forth your might,
Oh! hands so happy to labour,
Oh! labour indeed most light.
I would I could shed my life-blood,
My life-blood! but no, not yet;
More needful the daily bread I earn
By shedding these drops of sweat.

'For Him Who maketh all things,

These plough-shares, I make to sell,
To support by my clumsy labours
Him Who doth "all things well."
Work on, then; labour manfully;
So doing thou gainest food,
For Him, thy Strength, thy Life, thy Hope,
For Him, thine only Good.'

Thus he speaks to himself as he chisels,
As he chisels, and hammers, and planes,
And hour flies by after hour,
Till already the daylight wanes.
And the birds peep in at the window
As they sing their even-song—
While working thus for the Son of God
The day has seemed not long.

'My Father! my dearest Father!
Leave now thy work for to-day.
The evening's rest approacheth,
Come here with thy Child to play.'
That voice called the world into being,
And through it were all things made;
'Tis the voice of his great Creator,
That thus sweetly 'Father' said.

The old man trembles with gladness,
His heart beats quick with delight,
As with a train of Seraphim
The Holy One comes in sight.
St. Joseph kneels down to adore Him,

But the little hand strokes his face,
And putting His arms around him,
He nestles in His Father's embrace.

The Divine Child saw full clearly
How that pure and spotless mind,
Within a form so fragile,
The Divinity could find.
So, to the faith Himself implanted,
He dare give this rich reward,
And the arm that long had labored
'Thrones th' Eternal son of God.

And the golden head caressingly,
Leans on St. Joseph's breast,
And the little arms so pressingly,
Urge him to take some rest;
And within those eyes reflected,
He sees a whole heaven of love,
While the long-lost bliss of Paradise,
Seems op'ning from above.

Oh, Joseph! saintly carpenter,
Well may thy bronzed cheek flush,
And earth's anxieties and cares
Sink in an endless hush.
To merit such distinction,
Who would not toil all day,
For surely no worldly monarch,
Could a service thus repay?

Ye, who drain the cup of pleasure,
Who of earth's joys take your fill,
Ye, who labour to gather treasure,
And remain unsatisfied still;
Ye kings, and earthly potentates,
Clad in purple, and silk, and gold,
Say! what think you of this story
Of the Carpenter of old?

Do you think that if you asked him
He'd exchange his joys for yours?
Do you think that for one instant
He would care for the world's applause?
Ah, no! his joy exceeded
Any joy that this world could bring,
One touch of those tiny fingers
Outweighed every earthly thing.

Oh, Joseph, great St. Joseph!
Thy disciple let me be;
Take me into thy silent workshop,
And teach me to work like thee;
Let not this false world's glamour
Any longer my soul enthral;
To th' Incarnate God of Heaven,
Let me offer all for all.

Oh, I long to toil for Jesus!
To spend my life, and be spent,
And I would that my every faculty
Henceforth to this end be bent.

In this Child—unknown and slighted,
Misjudged and held in derision!—
Oh, gain for me as strong a faith
As to thee, dear Saint, was given!

To know God in His disguises,
Belongs to the pure in heart,
Grant, then, that in thy purity
I too may have a part.
Thy guerdon has fired my ardour,
Oh, grant that the flame may last,
And that I may work unceasingly,
Till life's short day is past.

And then, oh blessed Joseph!
When the work is almost done,—
When the length'ning shadows warn me
Of the setting of my sun,—
St. Joseph, do not forget me,
But come to me then, I pray,
And bring thy sweet child Jesus
To bid me with Him stay.

APPENDIX.

A Notice on the Cord of St. Joseph.

I.—ITS ORIGIN.

THE devotion to the Cord of St. Joseph took its rise in the town of Antwerp (Belgium), in the year 1657, in consequence of a miraculous cure effected by the wearing of this precious girdle.

At the above epoch there lived at Antwerp an Augustinian nun remarkable for her piety, called Sister Elizabeth, who, during three years, had suffered excruciating pains, occasioned by a most cruel distemper. She had then reached such a stage that the physicians, seeing no recourse possible, declared her death to be inevitable, and fast approaching. Losing all hope in human aid, the Sister addressed herself to Heaven, and having always had a particular devotion to St. Joseph, she prayed him to intercede with our Lord for her recovery. At the same time she had a cord blessed in the Saint's honour, girded herself with it, and a few days after, as she was praying before his image, she found herself all of a sudden freed from pain. Those who knew the disease and its nature, in her instance, declared her recovery miraculous. An authentic act was drawn up in presence of a public notary, and a Protestant physician could not help proclaiming the truth.

This fact, related by the Bollandists, was admitted by the author of a 'Month of St. Joseph,' published at Rome in 1810. The reading of this book in 1842, in St. Nicholas's Church at Verona, where the devotion of the Month of March was beginning to be practised, brought to the knowledge of several persons the event above related. Immediately, in imitation of the religious of Antwerp, many patients, animated by a tender piety towards St. Joseph, procured a cord blessed in the Church of St. Nicholas, where there is a chapel (since become a celebrated sanctuary) consecrated to the Saint.

Numerous special graces were obtained, and the devotion soon spread rapidly. Hundreds of cords were dispatched to France, Belgium, all parts of Italy, and even to America and Asia.

The Cord of St. Joseph was asked, not merely as a remedy against bodily ailments, but also as a preservative of the virtue of purity. Ere long, his lordship the Bishop of Verona became aware of the necessity of addressing a supplication to the Congregation of Rites, which he did by a letter bearing date January 14th, 1859. After a mature examination the Sacred Congregation, in accordance with the request, approved, by a Rescript of September 19, 1859, the new formula of blessing, and permitted its solemn and private use. Finally, his lordship obtained for the Association of the Cord of St. Joseph the privilege of being declared 'primarie,' and at the same time His Holiness Pope Pius IX. enriched it with precious indulgences.

II.—Graces Attached to the Wearing of the Cord of St. Joseph.

Graces precious to the piety of St. Joseph's servants are attached to the wearing of his cord. They are:—1st, St. Joseph's special protection; 2, purity of soul; 3, the grace of chastity; 4, final perseverance; 5, particular assistance at the hour of death.

III.—Nature of the Cord and Manner of Wearing it.

The Cord of St. Joseph should be of thread or cotton, ending at one extremity in seven knots, indicative of the joyful, dolorous, and glorious mysteries of the august Patriarch.

It is worn as a girdle, and ought to be blessed by a priest possessing powers to engird one with it.

IV.—Prayers of the Holy Cord.

Recite daily in honour of St. Joseph seven times Gloria Patri, together with the following prayer:

O St. Joseph, Father and Protector of Virgins, to whose faithful custody Christ Jesus, Innocence itself, and Mary Virgin of Virgins, were committed; I pray and beseech thee by these dear pledges Jesus and Mary, that being preserved from all uncleanness, I may with spotless mind, pure heart, and chaste body, ever most chastely serve Jesus and Mary all the days of my life. Amen.

V.—Plenary Indulgences attached to the Cord of St. Joseph.

1. On the day of entrance into the Association.
2. On the day of the Feast of the Espousals of the Blessed Virgin and St. Joseph (January 23rd).
3. On the 19th of March, the Feast of St. Joseph, and on one of the seven days which immediately follow that festival.
4. On the Patronage of St. Joseph (3rd Sunday after Easter).

5. At the article of death, for all the Associates who, being truly penitent, and having confessed their sins, shall receive the Holy Viaticum; or who, not being able to do this, shall invoke with the mouth or at least with the heart the Name of Jesus.

CONDITIONS FOR GAINING THE SAID INDULGENCES.

1. To be truly contrite, and to confess and communicate.
2. To visit the church or chapel of the Association or any other church or public oratory.
3. To pray there for peace between Christian princes, the extirpation of heresies, and the exaltation of our holy Mother the Church.

The plenary indulgence of a privileged altar is attached to all Masses celebrated for a departed Associate.

An indulgence of seven years and seven quarantines on each of the Sundays which come immediately after the Ember Saturdays for the Associates who shall visit with a contrite heart the church of the Arch-Confraternity, and there pray for the intentions of the Sovereign Pontiff.

All these indulgences are applicable to the souls in Purgatory.

Persons who are desirous of possessing one of the above Cords can apply to R. and T. Washbourne, Ltd., Paternoster Row, London. Price 6d., post free 7d.

FINIS.

Printed in Great Britain
by Amazon